A Life Worth Leading

0-8066-4998-4 John McCullough Bade
Will I Sing Again? Listening for the Melody of Grace in the Silence of Illness and Loss

0-8066-4988-7 Richard F. Bansemer
Getting Ready for the New Life: Facing Illness or Death with the Word and Prayers

0-8066-4991-7 D. Michael Bennethum
Listen! God Is Calling! Luther Speaks of Vocation, Faith, and Work

0-8066-4935-6 David A. Brondos
The Letter and the Spirit: Discerning God's Will in a Complex World

0-8066-5174-1 Eric Burtness
Leading on Purpose: Intentionality and Teaming in Congregational Life

0-8066-4992-5 Michael L. Cooper-White
On a Wing and a Prayer: Faithful Leadership in the 21st Century

0-8066-4995-X Barbara DeGrote-Sorensen & David Allen Sorensen
Let the Servant Church Arise!

0-8066-4936-4 Robert Driver-Bishop
People of Purpose: 40 Life Lessons from the New Testament

0-8066-4999-2 Rochelle Melander & Harold Eppley
Our Lives Are Not Our Own: Saying "Yes" to God

0-8066-5161-X Norma Cook Everist
Open the Doors and See All the People: Stories of Church Identity and Vocation

0-8066-4596-2 Kelly A. Fryer
Reclaiming the "L" Word: Renewing the Church from Its Lutheran Core

0-8066-4989-5 Ann E. Hafften
Water from the Rock: Lutheran Voices from Palestine

0-8066-4990-9 Susan K. Hedahl
Who Do You Say That I Am? 21st Century Preaching

0-8066-4997-6 Mary E. Hinkle
Signs of Belonging: Luther's Marks of the Church and the Christian Life

0-8066-5172-5 Robert F. Holley & Paul E. Walters
Called by God to Serve: Reflections for Church Leaders

0-8066-8001-6 Timothy F. Lull
On Being Lutheran

0-8066-4994-1 Martin E. Marty
Speaking of Trust: Conversing with Luther about the Sermon on the Mount

0-8066-4987-9 Cynthia Moe-Lobeda
Public Church: For the Life of the World

0-8066-4996-8 Carolyn Coon Mowchan & Damian Anthony Vraniak
Connecting with God in a Disconnected World: A Guide for Spiritual Growth and Renewal

0-8066-4993-3 Craig L. Nessan
Give Us This Day: A Lutheran Proposal for Ending World Hunger

0-8066-4934-8 Alvin Rogness
Living in the Kingdom: Reflections on Luther's Catechism

0-8066-5111-3 William Russell
Praying for Reform: Luther, Prayer, and the Christian Life

0-8066-5173-3 Joseph Sittler
Gravity and Grace: Reflections and Provocations

See www.lutheranvoices.com

LUTHERAN VOICES

A Life Worth Leading

Eric Burtness

Augsburg Fortress

Minneapolis

A LIFE WORTH LEADING

Large-quantity purchases or custom editions of these books are available at a discount from the publisher. For more information, contact the sales department at Augsburg Fortress, Publishers, 1-800-328-4648, or write to: Sales Director, Augsburg Fortress, Publishers, P.O. Box 1209, Minneapolis, MN 55440-1209.

Editor: Scott Tunseth

Cover Design: © Koechel Peterson and Associates, Inc., Minneapolis, MN
            www.koechelpeterson.com

Cover photo: Royalty-Free/Corbis. Used by permission.

Library of Congress Cataloging-in-Publication Data
Burtness, Eric, 1955-
  A life worth leading / Eric Burtness.
      p. cm.
  Includes bibliographical references.
  ISBN 0-8066-8000-8 (pbk. : alk. paper)
  1. Christian life. I. Title.
  BV4501.3.B89 2006
  248.4—dc22   2005037190

10   09   08   07   06   1   2   3   4   5   6   7   8   9   10

This book is dedicated to the memory of my older brother,
Stephen Christopher Burtness (1953-2005),
who taught those who knew him
about the purpose and meaning of life and love.

Contents

Introduction 9

1. The Power of Purpose 22

2. Worship: The Power to Inspire. 35

3. Fellowship: The Purpose of Integration 48

4. Discipleship: The Passion to Become Like Christ 57

5. Ministry: The Process of Involvement 68

6. Evangelism: The Importance of Inviting 79

7. One More Night with the Frogs 88

8. A Life Worth Leading 97

Endnotes 106

Introduction

For surely I know the plans I have for you, says the LORD,
plans for your welfare and not for harm,
to give you a future with hope.

When you search for me, you will find me;
if you seek me with all your heart, I will let you find me,
says the LORD.
    —Jeremiah 29:11, 13-14

He leadeth me O blessed thought;
O words with heavenly comfort fraught
Whate'er I do where-e'er I be, Still 'tis God's hand that leadeth me

He leadeth me, he leadeth me, By his own hand he leadeth me.
His faithful follower I would be, For by his hand he leadeth me.
    —Joseph H. Gilmore

"I had the pills in my mouth."

Trista had the pills in her mouth.

Trista was a loner who grew up without a lot of friends. In middle school she felt left out of many of the social groups. She struggled with a borderline eating disorder and depression. She didn't have anyone to confide in, no one she felt she could really talk to or share her troubles with. She felt like nobody cared whether she lived or died, and that included her only friend. Night after night

Trista cried herself to sleep, and she always kept her room dark to reflect the darkness of her soul.

Trista started planning her suicide carefully. She took pills from the family medicine cabinet over a period of time so that no one would notice. She planned to use them when she knew there was no point in continuing her life.

When the time came, Trista put the pills in her mouth and was reaching for the glass of water to swallow them just as the phone rang. Instinctively, she took the pills out and answered the phone. The voice on the line was Trista's one and only friend. "Trista, I needed to tell you that my uncle died." The two talked, and after a long conversation, her friend said, "Thanks, Trista. I don't know what I'd do without you."

The Sunday following this phone call, Trista came to church, and the sermon was on keeping a perspective on God's purpose for your life. Trista felt God speaking to her. Trista later told me, "I realized that life is more than going to school and eating and sleeping. I realized that I need to reach out to people who are going through difficult times in their lives."

Trista threw herself into church life. The youth director took Trista under her wing and helped lift her from the pits of despair. Trista began to realize that she could have a positive self-image. In high school she met Matt, whom she dated and married several years later. Trista has worked in our church nursery, has been a part of our praise worship team for eight years, and at the time this is being written is a student at Trinity Bible College with plans to go to seminary and be a pastor.

In the midst of a deep place of despair, Trista discovered meaning, purpose, and direction. She saw God's purpose for her life. Not everyone in Trista's situation is so fortunate.

A different perspective

A man returned from the funeral of a coworker who had died suddenly. "George" had been to the funeral because he felt obliged to go with several other people from his work to pay their respects. In the two weeks that followed the funeral, the man who had died was replaced by a new employee who took his old office, his house was sold, and his wife went to live in another city. The situation reminded George of what happens when a rock falls into a pool of water. For a few seconds it makes ripples in the water, but then the ripples dissipate. The rock has disappeared, and everything returns to what it was like before.

George was troubled by this and went to talk with his pastor. "I can't stop thinking that this could happen to me; that one day I will be here and a few days later I will be forgotten as if I had never lived. Shouldn't our lives," he somberly asked his pastor, "have more meaning and purpose than that?"[1]

Do you ever think about that? Do you ever have those haunting fears or a deep-down anxiety that you will have lived your whole life, but that your life will not have mattered? Do you ever have those worries that you will have worked all your life chasing a dream, only to retire and concede that the dream that you worked for simply didn't materialize, and you have nothing to look forward to except the daily reminder that you failed in your dream? Are you ever haunted by the fear that one day, when you die, the earth will swallow up your body and, along with it, any memory of any contribution that you have made to this life? Carl Jung once said that about a third of the people he counseled were not suffering from any clinically definable neurosis, but rather from the feeling that their lives were senseless and insignificant.

It's systemic and pervasive in our high-expectation, high-stress culture. We're doing more, producing more, and filling our days with activities, often not taking the chance to reflect deeply on the meaning and purpose of our lives.

Katie Brazelton in *Pathway to Purpose for Women* writes,

> Through my own faltering steps and my interaction with thousands of other women, I have come to realize that countless good, Christian women barely function because they feel alone, disillusioned, or trapped by vague dissatisfaction. They feel that they have no critically important reason to exist, and they are guilt-ridden about their dark secret of borderline despair.[2]

Do you ever wonder about the meaning and purpose of your life? Do you ever ask yourself questions like this:

- Where are you leading me, God? What do you want me to do with my life?
- What can I do to make a difference in someone's life?
- Why am I unsatisfied when I go to church and hear nice theological truths that don't relate to my everyday struggles?
- Why do I have such great plans but can never follow through on them?
- If I knew what God really wanted me to do with my life, would I have the time or the emotional energy to do it?

James White writes this in *You Can Experience a Purposeful Life:* "Contrary to popular belief, I don't think that our greatest fear is death. We all know we're going to die, but none of us believe it will ever happen. No, when we quiet ourselves and reflect on what matters most, I think our greatest fear is a wasted life. And our greatest hope? It's the opposite—a purposeful life."[3]

He continues by saying that most people live their lives on one of three levels. The first level is *survival*. They get up, go to work, punch the clock, spend their days, punch the clock, get home, watch TV, go to bed, and get up the next morning and do the whole routine over and over again. T.G.I.F. (Thank God It's Friday) comes from the survival mode of living. Instead of waking up and saying, "Good morning, Lord!" they wake up and say "Good Lord, it's morning." They live for the moment, and life simply consists of the accumulation of days.

A second level is the level of *success*. Those who focus on success want to make it big, with a big salary, a big house, and a big car. But focusing on material success is never fully satisfying, because there's always one more thing they need to confirm their image of success. Accumulation and materialism are hallmarks of the success level.

The third level is the level of *significance*. Significance can be found by discovering and living out one's life purpose. Living out the purpose for which God created you leads to a life worth leading. This is the level of living that we'll be exploring in this book. Through it I hope and pray you will make discoveries about the significant way in which you can live and lead your life.

Some biblical examples

Many people in the Bible found and followed the purpose for which God created them, and they lived with significance. One notable example is David, the son of a shepherd, who became the king who united the Nation of Israel in one of its most influential times. David's significance is summed up in the book of Acts with these words: "For David, after he had served the purpose of God in his own generation, died" (13:36).

"He served God's purpose and he died"—that's a pretty good epitaph to put on your tombstone! The people with the highest impact on their worlds are not always the most successful or the ones who possess the best titles or jobs. Rather, high impact people are often those who have discovered and followed God's purpose for their life.

Jeremiah, the "weeping prophet" of the Old Testament, is a wonderful example of someone who lived out God's purpose no matter what got in his way. He was a passionate prophet who was filled with sorrow for his people, and he consistently called them to repentance so that they could claim the legacy of David and Solomon. We learn several lessons from Jeremiah.

First, Jeremiah's purpose was rooted in God's call. God called Jeremiah when he was young, saying, "Before I formed you in the womb I knew you, and before you were born I consecrated you; I appointed you a prophet to the nations" (Jeremiah 1:5). God affirmed that call repeatedly throughout the book of Jeremiah (see Jeremiah 3:12; 7:2, 27-28; 11:2, 6; 13:12-13; 17:19-20). Is it possible for you to think that God had a purpose for you long before you were ever born? God didn't plan out all the minute details about the shoes you would wear or the house you would live in, but God does have a purpose for your life that is rooted in God's call.

Second, Jeremiah protested but God persisted. Jeremiah said, "Ah, Lord God! Truly I do not know how to speak, for I am only a boy" (Jeremiah 1:6). God addressed Jeremiah's concern by putting the words in his mouth, even though Jeremiah thought he was too young and too inexperienced. "Then the Lord put out his hand and touched my mouth; and the Lord said to me, 'Now I have put my words in your mouth'" (Jeremiah 1:9). You might think that God doesn't have a purpose for your life, or you may protest what God has placed in your heart as your life's purpose. But if you open your heart to what God wants to do with your life, you will enter into an amazing discovery process that will lead you beyond a life of success to a life of significance, a life worth leading.

Third, God warned Jeremiah that there would be troubles, but God would deliver him through them. God said, "They will fight against you; but they shall not prevail against you, for I am with you, says the Lord, to deliver you" (Jeremiah 1:19). Jeremiah was beaten, locked up in stocks, and publicly humiliated. The King cut up his writings and threw them in the fire. Jeremiah faced a multitude of troubles in life, but God had a purpose for Jeremiah. God said, "For surely I know the plans I have for you, says the Lord, plans for your welfare and not for harm, to give you a future with hope. . . . When you search for me, you will find me; if you seek me with all your heart, I will let you find me, says the LORD" (Jeremiah 29:11, 13-14). God had a purpose for Jeremiah that included a future with hope. God also promised him that if he sought God, he would be able to find God.

Do you believe that God has a purpose for your life? Do you believe that you can discover that purpose and live into it? It's possible to recognize that purpose and have a sense of vision for what living it out can look like, but if you lack a belief that it can happen, can that purpose be fulfilled? In part, it's about having a particular perspective on life. If you don't believe you can know it or discover it, you won't. The battle for knowing your purpose begins in your mind.

Remember Roger Bannister? It was a common belief for years that a human being could not run a mile in less than four minutes. It was thought to be humanly impossible, and sports writers said that his quest was preposterous. Medical experts produced studies that proved the feat was physically impossible. But Roger Bannister didn't believe the studies. He refused to let those barriers stand in his way. In the 1954 he did what the experts said could not be done—he made sports history, breaking the four minute barrier by running a mile in 3:59.4.

Within one year of Bannister shattering the record, thirty-two other athletes had broken the same four-minute barrier. Within ten years, 335 runners also beat that barrier. When asked how this could happen, Bannister answered that it was never a physical barrier, but a mental barrier. Once it was finally accomplished, hundreds of runners beat it because they were convinced that it was a breakable barrier.

The battle for discovering and knowing your purpose begins in your mind. If you think you can't know it, then you never will, and you've already lost the battle. But changing your life and discovering your purpose means being open to discovering God's purpose and to trusting the possibility that God can change your life.

The grasshopper complex

Let's think of a biblical example of changing your way of think-ing. The Old Testament book of Numbers is primarily a genealogi-cal book. There's not much "content" there, and very few Lutheran sermons are preached from Numbers. It only appears once in the three-year lectionary.

The book of Numbers is set in the time after Moses had led the people of Israel out of captivity in Egypt. The people had seen and experienced all kinds of wonders and miracles, including the parting of the Red Sea, water coming out of a rock, manna coming from heaven, and God leading them by a pillar of cloud and fire. They had experienced God's presence and sensed that God had a purpose for them.

In Numbers 13 they were encamped at an oasis just south of the Promised Land of Canaan. It was there that the Lord asked Moses to send spies into the land of Canaan to see if it was safe to enter. Each of the tribes of Israel chose one leader to go. Moses charged the leaders to go into the land and see what the land was like, what kind of people lived there, and whether the land was rich or poor. Moses also asked them to be bold and bring back some fruit of the land.

For forty days the spies surveyed the land, and they did bring back some fruit from the Promised Land: "And they came to the Wadi Eshcol, and cut down from there a branch with a single cluster of grapes, and they carried it on a pole between two of them. They also brought some pomegranates and figs" (Numbers 13:23). Think of that! Normally you can hold a cluster of grapes in your hand. But the land flowing with milk and honey grew grapes so huge that they only brought back a single cluster hung on a pole that it took two men to carry! And they brought back "some" pomegranates and figs, presumably also because of their huge size. This was indeed the incredible land that God had promised they could inherit. This was God's purpose for them.

The spies reported to Moses and the people of Israel: "We came to the land to which you sent us; it flows with milk and honey, and this is its fruit. Yet, the people who live in the land are strong. . . ." (Numbers 13:27-28). The fruit of the land was incredible, but the report was not all positive. Notice the word *yet* at the beginning of the sentence. Like the word *but*, the word *yet* negates what was said before. Yes, the land was flowing with milk and honey, "yet the people who live in the land are strong, and the towns are fortified and very large." The spies go on to report: "We are not able to go up against this people, for they are stronger than we. . . . The land that we have gone through as spies is a land that devours its inhabitants; and all the people that we saw in it are of great size. There we saw the Nephalim . . ." (Numbers 13:28, 31-33).

And then they said these words of despair: ". . . and to ourselves we seemed like grasshoppers, and so we seemed to them" (Numbers 13:33).

Ten of the spies had the "grasshopper complex." They didn't focus on the potential that Moses asked them to explore; instead, they focused on the problems they thought they were going to face: "To ourselves we seemed like grasshoppers, and so we seemed to them." They saw only problems and not the potential of the Promised Land. They approached the future with fear instead of faith. They looked at the giants instead of keeping their eyes on God. Their message to Moses was that the challenges were too big for them. Their lack of faith also showed they believed the challenges were too big for God.

Think of the challenges in your life. God is calling you and challenging you to do one or many things. God has given you incredible promises, and God promises to stick with you and to help you live out your calling through any challenges you might face. Those who recognize God's purpose for their lives but don't trust that they are up to the task are living out the grasshopper complex. But God calls us to keep our eyes on God and move forward. No matter how giant the task (remember the Nephalim), God also promises to walk beside us.

Caleb: Following God wholeheartedly

The story of Numbers continues. In Numbers 14 the people started to complain against Moses, saying that they wanted to go back to Egypt, back to the good old days when they were in captivity, where at least they knew the ground rules! Rather than trusting God to move their lives forward in faith, they wanted to retreat in fear.

But Joshua and Caleb (the two spies with a greater vision) tore their clothes and gathered the assembly and said, "The land that we went through as spies is an exceedingly good land. If the LORD is pleased with us, he will bring us into this land and give it to us, a land that flows with milk and honey. Only, do not rebel against the LORD; and do not fear the people of the land . . . the LORD is with us; do not fear them" (Numbers 14:7-9).

Through the rest of Numbers 14, God got angry and threatened to disinherit the people of Israel. Moses interceded for them, reminding God that the LORD is slow to anger and abounding in steadfast love. God did forgive their rebellion, but it came with a price. The people would wander in the wilderness for forty years (one year for each day the spies spent in the Promised Land), and none of the people who were in that generation would see the Promised Land except for Joshua and Caleb. Listen to what God said about Caleb: "But my servant Caleb, because he has a different spirit and has followed me wholeheartedly, I will bring into the land into which he went, and his descendents shall possess it" (Numbers 14:24).

The people faced forty more years of wilderness wanderings because they believed the spies who said that God was not up to the challenges that lay before them. The vision of the future was right in front of them, staring them in the face, but the people did not trust it could happen. They looked at themselves and saw only grasshoppers, rather than relying on the giant promises that God had given them.

It's my conviction that Christians fall into one of three categories. Some are in captivity to a variety of habits or addictions or attitudes that keep them enslaved to lifestyles and are stuck in a kind of self-made bondage. Like the people who wanted to return to Egypt, they seek comfort in an enslaving situation or relationship. They know that a better vision and a greater purpose is out there for them, but they are afraid to step forward into God's new future. All of us experience this at one time or another, and recognizing that particular bondage or fear is the first step in discovering a new calling or purpose.

Many other Christians are in a second category of wandering in the wilderness without a specific sense of purpose or vision or direction. They know that there's a life that God has promised them, yet it's not theirs to possess. The *yet* negates the promise.

Christians in a third category display a different spirit. They follow God wholeheartedly, and, like Caleb, are able to enter the Promised Land of God's purpose for their lives. Take some time today to consider where you are. Are you in bondage in Egypt? Are you wandering in the wilderness? Or are you like Caleb, with a different spirit that follows God wholeheartedly?

A guide through the wilderness

This book was written for those wandering in the wilderness, wondering about God's purpose for your life, and not yet experiencing that purpose. Those in captivity may need a different kind of book. Those already in the Promised Land know the blessings of a purposeful life. But most Christians, I believe, are wandering in the wilderness and need a guide to get through to the Promised Land of God's purpose for their lives.

This book is meant to be used in a variety of ways. Read it independently as a resource to encourage you to find your life purpose and then live it with passion. It can also be read it with a small group at church or with another group with whom you are comfortable.

Use one chapter each time you meet, and use the additional resources for small group discussion that are available at www.alifeworthleading.org.

A third way to use this book is as a five-to-eight-week congregational emphasis during which your entire congregation can discover what it means to live a life worthy of the calling to which you have been called. A sermon series can easily be constructed for each of the life purposes in chapters 3-7, and small groups within the congregation can gather, read this book, and answer the questions at the end of each chapter and use the added Web resources. Robert Driver-Bishop's book *People of Purpose* (Augsburg Fortress) can enhance personal daily devotions, as each chapter reflects on a different New Testament person of purpose. Visit www.alifeworthleading.org to see specific tie-ins with these two books and how they are intentionally aligned. On the Web site are also worship resources and sermons that have been preached in other congregations for this series.

If you have a congregational emphasis like this, be sure to consider Kelly Fryer's study called *No Experience Necessary*,[4] a wonderfully insightful way to see God at work in your life. Again, see the examples of how to utilize these resources fully along with sample sermons for a sermon series at www.alifeworthleading.org.

Leading on Purpose: Intentionality and Teaming in Congregational Life[5] is a book that will help you put these principles to work in the structural life of your congregation. There are also Web resources available for this book at www.leadingonpurpose.org.

Let's join together on a journey of a purposeful discovery. Let's seek to discover God's calling for your life.

Questions for discussion

1.   As you search for purpose in your life, are you in captivity (in Egypt), wandering (in the wilderness without purpose), or have you arrived (in the Promised Land)? How do you feel about where you are, and what do you want to do about it?

2.   Do you believe that the God has a purpose and a direction for your life? If so, what might it be? If not, what are the reasons you don't believe it?

3.   What is it that you want to get out of reading this book? Write it down on the inside cover and return to that after you finish the book.

1

The Power of Purpose

I came that they may have life, and have it abundantly.
    —John 10:10

Every man dies; not every man really lives!
    —William Wallace, from the movie *Braveheart*

What no eye has seen, nor ear heard,
nor the human heart conceived,
what God has prepared for those who love him.
    —1 Corinthians 2:9

Rick Warren's *The Purpose-Driven Life: What On Earth Am I Here For?*[1] has sold 22 million copies since being published in 2002. Pastor Warren leads one of the country's largest congregations, with weekend attendance of sixteen thousand. *The Purpose-Driven Life* is a byproduct of his *The Purpose-Driven Church,* written in 1995.

In both books Rick Warren focuses on the five biblical purposes set forth in the Great Commandment and the Great Commission:

"You shall love the Lord your God with all your heart, and with all your soul, and with all your mind. This is the greatest and first commandment. And a second is like it: You shall love your neighbor as yourself" (Matthew 22:37-39).

"Go therefore and make disciples of all nations, baptizing them in the name of the Father and of the Son and of the Holy Spirit, and teaching them to obey everything that I have commanded you" (Matthew 28:19-20).

Out of these verses come five purposes of the church:

- *Love the Lord our God* is worship, as we celebrate God's presence in worship.
- *Baptizing them* is fellowship, as we incorporate God's family through fellowship.
- *Teaching them* is discipleship, as we educate God's people through discipleship.
- *Love your neighbor as yourself* is ministry, as we demonstrate God's love through ministry.
- *Go and make disciples* is evangelism, as we communicate God's Word through evangelism.[2]

In *The Purpose-Driven Life* Rick Warren tells us that these are not only purposes for the church, but purposes for our lives.

Worship means that we were planned for God's pleasure. Warren says that the biblical word for loving God is *worship*. When we receive the loving and gracious gifts that God wants to give us, that's worship.

Fellowship means that we were formed for God's family. The Bible tells us that we can't really make it through the Christian life without being a part of a church family. Fellowship in the church makes it a living organism, rather than a lifeless organization.

Discipleship means that we were created to become like Christ. It means thinking like Jesus, feeling like Jesus, and acting like Jesus. It's a trilogy that touches the head, heart, and hands. Using different words, it has to do with the mind, will, and conduct, or our convictions, character, and conduct. Discipleship is not only learning. It is *doing* everything in the name of Jesus.

Ministry means that we were shaped for serving God. God calls each of us to have a ministry in the church and a mission in the world. As we come closer to discovering God's purpose for our lives, our ministry of serving becomes even clearer.

Evangelism means that we were made for a mission. One of the insights Warren points out is that your circle of influence with your family, friends, and neighbors is a very unique circle. Nobody in the world has that same circle that you do. *Evangelism* means that you are called to reach out to certain people through the use of your unique gifts.

Discerning how to balance these five purposes in our personal lives is a way in which we can discover the purpose for which God has created us.

Critiques of Warren's theology

Since *The Purpose-Driven Life* has become so popular, Warren has attracted much positive and negative critique. Some of the theological critiques are valid for those who have a different perspective. Rick Warren is a Southern Baptist, so there are obvious theological differences from our Lutheran convictions.

Some of the critiques have to do with a superficial theology and incomplete doctrinal references. He lacks reference to repentance or to the eternal consequence of sin. His commitment prayer, "Jesus, I believe in you and receive you," emphasizes grace without a full understanding of the depravity of humanity or original sin. He emphasizes God's love, but not God's wrath.

Other critiques have to do with Warren's use of Scripture in his books. There are over twelve hundred scriptural references from more than a dozen different translations and paraphrases. Many times his use of Scripture seems to be simple "proof texting" and taking certain verses out of context. Bible verses that have to do with the cross, our sinful nature, absolute truth, or the sovereignty of God often are de-emphasized, while issues of love, family, and spiritual success are emphasized.

Still other critiques have to do with the market-driven mindset that promises happiness through what the Christian life can do for you. Rick Warren writes, "Knowing God's purpose for creating you will reduce your stress, focus your energy, simplify your decisions, give meaning to your life, and, most important, prepare you for eternity."[3] Some have dismissed Warren's writings as being too consumer oriented with doctrine that is far too shallow.

Probably the criticism that is most challenging theologically for Lutherans is that Warren's material is too focused on sanctification instead of justification. For Lutherans, justification by grace through faith is the cornerstone of our distinctive understanding of the Christian faith. We tend to be shy about speaking of sanctification. We'll be addressing that in a later chapter.

Most of these criticisms and critiques have a degree of validity. Some Lutheran churches have chosen not to use Warren's material at all because of critiques like these. Many other Lutheran congregations have "Lutheranized" the material in study groups by using Luther's Small Catechism alongside Warren's material and have experienced a deepening of people's faith and commitment.

Over one thousand Lutheran churches (including LCMS) have participated in the Warren's "40 Days of Purpose" campaigns over the past several years. The campaign utilizes weekend worship, sermons, music, small group video discussion guides, and a great variety of Internet resources in order to tailor make the campaign for a particular congregation. You can find out much more about the "40 Days of Purpose" campaigns at Saddleback's site at www.purposedriven.com. For an excellent site with many Lutheran resources see www.purposedrivenlutherans.com. You can also find Lutheran resources at www.leadingonpurpose.org.

Transformation experiences

Many Lutheran churches and their people have experienced transformation congregations and personal lives through a "40 days" type of campaign that utilizes a unique style of preaching and teaching and the positive emphasis on living your life's purpose.

Dave Wasemann is the pastor of Christus Victor in Manassas, Virginia. Dave has thoroughly integrated the purpose-driven style of ministry into the congregation's teaching, preaching, and programming. Wayne, a member of Christus Victor, leads a Lutheran Men in Mission group along with a Mission Transformation ministry team. At first he was skeptical about becoming involved in the 40 Days Campaign, partially because Rick Warren is Baptist, and Wayne has been a Lutheran all his life. He knew he had differences with Warren's theology, but Pastor Dave encouraged him to give it a try. Wayne was deeply drawn into *The Purpose-Driven Life* and found that Warren's use of different Bible translations was not distracting; in fact, it enhanced his reading of the material. He said, "The different translations were one of the most positive things, as they offer a different slant. When I hear 'In the beginning was the Word,' I know exactly what comes next. But with different translations you think about it in a new way."

Wayne felt called into the ministry when he was young, but he had his doubts about preaching and teaching and leading a congregation. Instead of going into the ministry, he went to William and Mary College and spent his life in public education, most recently as a principal at an elementary school in Prince William County, outside of Fairfax, Virginia.

Now in retirement, Wayne has discovered in Pastor Dave's sermons and, in participating in the 40 Days Campaign, a new sense of purpose in his life. Wayne felt drawn back into ministry as a hospice caregiver or a diaconal minister. His devotional time is spent reading both the Bible and *The Purpose-Driven Life* where he finds stories of how people were empowered by God to discover their life's purpose. Each time he reads it, he underlines more Bible verses and insights.

As Wayne struggled with whether or not he should go to seminary after his retirement as a grade school principal, he often asked God in his prayers whether or not this was just a personal quest that he was pursuing, or whether it was a call from God. On the last day of class at the school picnic, a man told Wayne that he used some of the profits from a small computer company he owned to support an African mission. But when he heard that Wayne was planning to go to seminary, the man said that he wanted to support Wayne's seminary education. Wayne didn't feel comfortable accepting the generous offer, but he went back into school and thanked God for bringing a word from this man.

Wayne has started taking classes at Gettysburg Seminary on the diaconal minister track. God has put in his heart the knowledge that we're all given gifts by God and that we need to take the opportunity to share those gifts with others. Wayne is living into his life's purpose.

Prayer shawls revisited

In *Leading on Purpose* I told the story of Nita, a woman in our congregation who started a prayer shawl ministry, significant ministry that started when God knocked on the door of Nita's heart.

Nita began the prayer shawl ministry in August 2003. During the first year 133 shawls were crafted and given as gifts. By August 2005 a total of 357 have been gifted—224 in the second year. Nita leads a group of thirty-five dedicated women who prayerfully, lovingly, and freely give of their resources, time, and talents.

The really remarkable thing is that fourteen other congregations have begun prayer shawl ministries with Nita's help, and Nita's team welcomes them and prays for them as they begin work in this mission field. When I asked Nita what this ministry has meant to her she said the following:

I sometimes question why I have been so blessed to have the opportunity to lead this small group, purpose driven ministry. Having been involved in many different areas of the church over the years, I had taken a "backseat" for a period of time. I wouldn't say that I was burned out, but taking a hiatus while being in prayer about where I needed to serve God. Having been a participant in a week-long workshop lead by Rick Warren in 1999, I knew about purpose-driven ministry and the belief that where there is a passion, a ministry will thrive. I prayed about what my passion really was and how to combine it in a Christian-based activity. I prayed about how I should spend my time.

God does answer prayer and frequently in amazing ways! I now spend my time in the Prayer Shawl ministry, and I am so blessed by it. I am stretched and strengthened each day by the ministry. I learn daily more about the Holy Spirit in my life. I am better at prayer, and I am amazed at the places I have gone while being led by the Holy Spirit.

Nita drew from some of her life's experience to discover this purpose for her life. As a young girl she had learned how to knit. While she was in high school she was involved in the speech team and learned valuable communication skills. As a young adult she learned through her Myers Briggs Type Indicator® (a tool to help one recognize personality preferences) that one of her primary traits was being an encourager. And now, in her late 50s, she has been able to put all three of those parts of her life together in this ministry. It has deepened her faith and brought her closer to God's heart.

Nita has truly found her purpose, and God has blessed her abundantly. It has given her a window for service. Through the Holy Spirit, God's grace has tugged on her heart to step out and do things she normally would shy away from. "I know that being in this ministry has transformed me in ways that I can't even identify with words," Nita said. "It is the Holy Spirit transforming me, and I am blessed to be one of the everyday and ordinary people to share God's love and grace through the knitting and gifting of the prayer shawls."

It's not about you

Rick Warren begins *The Purpose-Driven Life* with these words: "It's not about you."

> The purpose of your life is far greater than your own personal fulfillment, your peace of mind, or even your happiness. It's far greater than your family, your career, or even your wildest dreams and ambitions. If you want to know why you were placed on this planet, you must begin with God. You were born by his purpose and for his purpose.[4]

Now, it's true that passionate and purposeful lives like Wayne's and Nita's are very fulfilling and satisfying. It is not without pain, trouble, or difficulties, though a life with purpose brings a wonderful feeling of significance and satisfaction. But that's not the point; it isn't about our sense of accomplishment. I know that Nita is only humbled by what God has done through her. She knows that it's about God, bringing glory to God, and sharing God's life and love with others.

In our Lutheran Church, some would describe this as sanctification. When we hear God calling and we respond in service, we practice a new kind of obedience. Does that obedience "gain us" salvation? No, but it does lead to new life, a life that is more in line with God's purposes for us. A life worth leading is one that combines belief with behavior. What we believe is inextricably connected to how we behave. They can be distinguished, but they should not be separated. This is different from some of the critiques of Warren's writings as "works righteousness" which says that we're saved by our works, and not by God's grace.

Living our lives in accordance with God's will is a part of the foundation of the Lutheran faith, and it changes your life. Sanctification is a part of our Lutheran heritage.

Kelly Fryer, assistant professor of congregational leadership at Luther Seminary in St. Paul, Minnesota, tells of a time she asked a class of sixty seminary students if they could think of a single person in the Bible who had an encounter with God and went away unchanged. They couldn't think of anyone, though someone suggested Judas. Then it was pointed out that when Judas went out and hung himself he certainly had experienced a major change, but it was not a positive one!

Fryer writes that change is a "certain outcome of an encounter with God. We are different people because God is in our lives."[5] She continues:

> Those sixteenth-century Lutheran reformers were so certain of this that they built it into the structure of their main document, the Augsburg Confession. Composed of a number of articles of faith, the document sums up their ideas about God and the church and the Christian life. The first few articles basically say that God created everything and we keep messing it up. Article 4 describes God's amazing gift of love and our salvation through Jesus Christ. Article 5 discusses the way in which this gift comes to us in the Word of God. And Article 6 (are you ready for this?!) tells us that the first fruit of salvation is a changed life. In other words, we expect something to happen in a life once Jesus is in it. There is a change. There is conversion. There is transformation.[6]

That transformation is sanctification. Article 6 of the Augsburg Confession, "Concerning the New Obedience" clearly states the importance of obedience and behavior as a response of faith, though not as a way of salvation. Part of the struggle for many Lutherans is how to see how a Christian life of response fits into the Lutheran conviction that we are saved by grace through faith.

Ephesians 2:8 reads this way: "For by grace you have been saved through faith, and this is not your own doing; it is the gift of God—not the results of works, so that no one may boast." That's the quintessential Lutheran Bible verse. But the verse continues, "For we are what he has made us, created in Christ Jesus for good works, which God prepared beforehand to be our way of life." By grace you have been saved through faith, and you were created in Christ Jesus for good works, which God prepared beforehand to be your way of life.

Paul talks about three components here: We are saved *by* grace *through* faith *for* good works. Paul is not opposed to good works; he's simply interested in getting the order right! You're not saved by works for faith, nor saved by grace without faith, but you are saved *by* grace, *through* faith, *for* good works. The order is important, and all three prepositions are important in their proper order.

In the same way that many Lutherans have trouble with sanctification, they have even more trouble with the letter of James! That should be no surprise, since Luther himself questioned the wisdom of including the book of James in the New Testament. Partly because the name of Jesus is mentioned only twice and because there are no references at all to the resurrection of Jesus, Martin Luther referred to the book of James as a "straw epistle." Some scholars have designated James as the least "Lutheran" book of the Bible, because James states that faith without works is dead. Since many Lutherans have an aversion to talking about good works, James is seen as being oriented toward works, and not toward grace. Some scholars claim that James' theological orientation delayed its acceptance in the final list of New Testament books until the final years before the list as we know it was settled.

But the value of the letter of James is that he talks about real faith for real life, a phrase that happens to be the title of a book by Mike Foss, which I will reference several times.[7] James' intent was not to write with the theological depth of Paul. James' intent was to write a practical guide to help early Christians to live out their faith. We look for real things, like real coffee, or real leather, or Coke as the "real thing." James gives us insights into real faith for real life.

Let's think a little further about the difference between Paul and James. Paul says in Galatians 2:16 that "we know that a person is justified not by the works of the law, but through faith in Jesus Christ." James writes in chapter 2 that faith, without works, is dead. How do we hold together what Paul says when he says that we're justified through faith and not works, and James says that if you don't have works, your faith is dead?

Part of the answer lies in the different problems about which Paul and James were writing. The problem that Paul was dealing with was legalism. Paul was talking to a group of people who said that you had to keep all the Jewish laws and regulations to be a Christian. You had to be circumcised, eat some things and not others, and only then you could consider yourself Christian.

James was not dealing with the problem of legalism; he was dealing with the problem of Christian laziness. James was likely dealing with a group of Jewish Christians who had been in Jerusalem, but who started to suffer persecution after the stoning of Stephen. They then moved out of the supportive city where they had the fellowship of other Christians and back into surrounding towns and regions. The letter of James may have been written around AD 55, before all of Paul's letters were completed, and much before the Gospels of Matthew, Luke, and John were written. As these Jewish Christians started to disperse all around the Mediterranean Sea, they no longer had contact with the teachers and preachers who had nurtured them, and they started to think that it doesn't matter what you do, as long as you believe. James was not dealing with Paul's problem of legalism; he was dealing with the problem of laziness. James wants to emphasize that it matters a great deal what you do and how you live. What one believes is reflected in how one behaves.

Second, when Paul talks about *works* he is talking about the Jewish laws and regulations. When James talks about *works*, he's simply talking about a Christian lifestyle. As such, James would agree that we're saved by grace through faith for good works; in other words, for living a real faith in a real life.

Third, Paul's focus is more on the root of salvation and has to do with faith as something more internal and unseen. James doesn't focus on the root of salvation, but on the fruit of salvation in our lives. James is interested in acts of love that characterize the life of a Christian. Again, real faith for real life. That's what James is writing about.

And fourth, Paul's purpose is to focus on how to *know* that I'm a Christian. James' focus is how to *show* that I'm a Christian. Paul wants to focus on how to *become* a believer, and James wants to talk about how to *behave* as a believer. Paul and James are not contradictory; they are complementary. Paul wants to *know* Christ, and James wants to *show* Christ. *A Life Worth Leading* deals with God's purpose and how to show you're a Christian. It makes the connection between believing and behaving.

One important way to do that is to balance the five purposes of worship, fellowship, discipleship, ministry, and evangelism in your life. We need balance in our lives. We need a balance of food, exercise, and sleep to be healthy. We also need a balance of the five purposes in our lives to be spiritually healthy. As you read, take time to consider the questions at the end of each chapter and how it relates to your life.

We'll spend the next five chapters talking about God's five purposes for your life: worship, fellowship, discipleship, ministry, and evangelism.

Questions for discussion

1. What are you so passionate about that you would even do it without pay? What is your passion that only needs a little breeze to turn it into a raging fire? How could you find a way to use that passion for God's purpose for ministry or service?

2. If you could summarize the significance of your life in a five-word sentence, what would it be?

3. What have you done as a Christian that gives you the most fulfillment?

4. What do you think of the concept of "knowing you are a Christian and showing your Christian faith"? Do you agree or disagree that Paul's theology and James' theology are complementary?

2

Worship: The Power to Inspire

I appeal to you therefore, brothers and sisters,
by the mercies of God, to present your bodies as a living sacrifice,
holy and acceptable to God,
which is your spiritual worship.
　—Romans 12:1

Oh, come, let us worship and bow down,
let us kneel before the Lord, our Maker!
For he is our God, and we are the people of his pasture,
and the sheep of his hand.
　—Psalm 95:6-7

Have you ever experienced the following scenario? You wake up late for Sunday morning worship and run around the house getting the kids up and dressed and ready for Sunday school. As you drive to church, little Johnny keeps poking Molly in the back seat and violates the imaginary boundary line you've repeatedly drawn down the middle of the back seat to keep them separated. With a sigh of relief you get them to Sunday school late. You crave that cup of coffee, but when you get to church, they've just run out of the tepid brew that's usually served in Lutheran basement fellowship halls. Undaunted, you go to the Adult Forum to hear about the latest social issue, but the presenter doesn't show up and you end up being cornered by someone from the Church Council pressuring you to serve on the Stewardship Committee. You start to feel you'd rather be at the dentist. You pick up Johnny and Molly from Sunday school and find out that Johnny has spent the hour with the Sunday school superintendent because he swore at the teacher. On the way into worship your cell phone rings, and it's that pesky insurance guy who wants to sell you earthquake insurance. You've just about had it when you get to "your" pew—the one your family has occupied for four generations—and a visitor has had the gall to be sitting there. You think to yourself, "What a waste of time; I'm not going to get anything out of this."

Did you waste your time that morning?

Perhaps you did, if you were focusing on what *you* were doing.

But what was God about to do?

What if, during one of the hymns you were really touched by God's Spirit when you sang:

"Take my life, that I may be Consecrated, Lord, to thee.
Take my heart it is thy own. It shall be thy very own."
    —Frances R. Havergal

What if the whole worship experience boiled down to that one moment, when you faithfully realized what you needed to give in response to God's grace? Would it have been a wasted experience? What if you sang these words from your heart with your eyes closed as God spoke to you in worship:

Shout to the Lord, all the earth let us sing.
Power and majesty, praise to the king.
Mountains bow down and the seas will roar
At the sound of your name
I sing for joy at the work of your hands
Forever I'll love you, forever I'll stand
Nothing compares to the promise I have in you.
    —Darlene Zschech

What if you went to worship every Sunday intentionally looking for just one thing that God was wanting to say to you, just one way that God spoke to you to transform your life, or just one step closer to the will of God? We battle the constant temptation to conform our lives to the standards of the secular world around us. Present your body, head, heart, and hands to God. Present your convictions, your character, and your conduct to God as a living sacrifice. God will make it holy and acceptable. The Apostle Paul calls that your spiritual worship (Romans 12:1).

Worship: Your first purpose

For Lutherans, the primary focus of worship is what God is doing. God wants to transform our minds instead of having us give in to the temptation of being conformed to the world around us. Kelly Fryer writes: "The cross reminds us that it doesn't matter how well we pray, it only matters that a loving God hears our prayers. The cross reminds us that it doesn't matter how perfectly we sing in worship, it only matters that the Spirit of God is there with us in worship."[1]

Because of this it's important to realize that worship is not centered on what you like. It's centered on whom you love. Far too many Lutheran congregations have "worship wars" centered on the style of worship that people prefer. The music, the settings of the liturgy, or even the certain praise songs we sing are all a means to center on God. When our worship centers on God and God's word to us through preaching, song, and sacrament, the style or format is important but not ultimately more important than our focus on God.

Mike Foss writes that "worship is about the coming of God. In the midst of the Scripture reading, the preaching, and singing God shows up. In worship, people who long to connect with the Spirit can heal their heart's hunger."[2]

I've come to appreciate what Rick Warren says about Christian music. He writes that worship is not only for our benefit, it's for God's benefit. The style of worship that we prefer says more about us than it says about God. He writes, "Every part of a church service is an act of worship: praying, Scripture reading, singing, confession, silence, being still, listening to a sermon, taking notes, giving an offering, baptism, communion, signing a commitment card, and even greeting other worshipers."[3] Though it seems like a stretch for Lutherans, Warren also writes, "There is no such thing as 'Christian' music; there are only Christian lyrics. It is the words that make a song sacred, not the tune. There are no spiritual tunes. If I played a song for you without the words, you'd have no way of knowing if it were a 'Christian' song."[4]

God loves all kinds of music. Listen to some verses from Psalm 150:

Praise the Lord!
Praise him with trumpet sound;
Praise him with lute and harp!
Praise him with tambourine and dance,
Praise him with strings and pipe!
Praise him with clanging cymbals;
Praise him with loud clashing cymbals!
Let everything that breathes praise the Lord!
Praise the Lord!

Notice the loud clanging cymbals! God loves all kinds of music; but it's the lyrics that bring praise to God and can lift us to an experience of God's presence, whether it is traditional, praise, hip-hop, or rap. Now, please know that I personally have a little trouble with this. I can't imagine using Country Western-style lyrics in worship where people sing, "Drop kick me Jesus through the goal posts of life." It doesn't speak to my heart of worship, though I know there are Lutheran churches that have Country Western-worship services. It wouldn't be my choice, but that's fine. We need to let go of church fights about styles of worship, and begin focusing on words and experiences that bring those who worship closer to what God wants to offer.

Worship hymns and songs are written by poets, and not always systematic theologians. Most hymns contain at least some theological error: "'Twas grace that taught my heart to fear" may be an incorrect separation of law and gospel, but we all still sing "Amazing Grace." So, whether we use the *SBH, LBW, WOV,* or the new *ELW,* what matters is recognizing how God comes close to us in worship and how we can draw closer to God through whatever worship style we find at the congregation we attend.

Rick Warren writes that "The heart of worship is surrender. . . . It is the natural response to God's amazing love and mercy. We give ourselves to him, not out of fear or duty, but in love, *'because he first loved us.'*"[5] Worship as surrender means we recognize that the deep love of Jesus led him to the cross where he laid down his life for you and me. We deserve the suffering and death that Jesus experienced on the cross. We deserve it as punishment for our sins. But the gospel declares that Jesus went to the cross in our place as a sacrifice (Romans 3:23-25). His death paid our debt.

Several years ago, a little girl at the Stanford Medical Hospital was suffering from a rare and very serious disease. Her only chance of survival was receiving a complete blood transfusion. The doctors were convinced that the best chance of a blood transfusion would be from her five-year-old brother, who had miraculously survived the same disease and had developed antibodies to fight the disease. He would be her only hope. At five years old, the doctors knew that he couldn't understand everything that was going on, and so they just asked him if he would be willing to help out his big sister by giving her his blood. The little boy looked at the doctors, looked at his sister, and agreed to help.

As the little boy lay in the bed next to his sister and saw his blood starting to pass from his arm to hers, he looked up at the doctor and said with a trembling voice, "Will I start to die right away, or will it take a while?"

It was then that the doctors realized that he thought that he was giving his very life for his sister.[6]

In worship we gather to surrender ourselves totally to God, whose son Jesus chose to lay down his life for us on the cross. In worship we surrender ourselves to receive what God so graciously wants to give. In *People of Purpose*, Robert Driver-Bishop writes, "Worship involves an act of complete surrender to God. We do not worship for our own benefit. We worship to please God. During worship we do not pray, 'my will be done,' but 'God's will be done.' Worship is about completely surrendering to God's message and God's way of doing things."[7]

Beth's blessings

Beth, a member of St. Matthew Lutheran, has been an inspiration to me ever since I've become a pastor of the congregation. She's been a blessing not because everything has always gone well for her, but because in every situation that she's faced she finds the grace of God and receives it with thanks.

In June 2003 her husband, Chuck, was laid off work and continues (at age 58) to look for full-time employment. A week after he was laid off, Beth had to have a hysterectomy, and a week after that doctors discovered she had colon cancer in a fibroid. She received a prayer shawl from a friend, which caused her to contact Nita and encourage her to begin a prayer shawl ministry at St. Matthew (see chapter 1).

A month later she had colon resection to deal with her stage IV cancer. A month later she had a resection to remove cancer that had spread to the liver. This was followed by an infection on her incision that meant almost eight weeks of daily dressing changes performed by three nurses from the congregation. People from St. Matthew surrounded Beth and Chuck with love and support, as she couldn't vacuum or plant her geraniums. Forty meals were delivered, and over the next six months many different people brought her to the hospital for chemotherapy, often accompanied by a baked casserole, the third Lutheran sacrament (coffee is the fourth).

A year later Beth had a CT/PET scan that showed that her cancer had returned: a spot on her brain didn't look quite right. Further tests showed that it was "only" a brain aneurysm. She went to see her neurosurgeon who looked too young to be a doctor. She was delighted to find that her neurosurgeon was member of St. Matthew (an additional blessing!). The plan for treatment included putting a coil in her brain by going through a vessel in her groin and threading it through her body and into her brain.

Now, you need to know that Beth is the most passionate ministry person I know. She always finds ways to receive the blessings that God wants to give her, even through multiple challenges! Throughout the past difficult years she has developed a ministry of communicating with an amazing number of people. Beth has the spiritual gift of mass communication, though that's not listed on any spiritual gift inventory I've ever seen. Beth communicates about church life on the phone every day to more people than I talk to in a week. She initiated our e-mail ministry of weekly devotions on the Sunday texts, weekly news updates, and funeral notices that reach more than three hundred people. Additionally, she has the gift of a wonderful husband whom she met at Luther League 41 earlier. Chuck has loved her and supported her every step of the way. She calls him her "first class jewel," though she justifiably groans at his jokes. Both of them worship God not only on Sunday mornings, but also as their way of life.

Knowing and loving Beth as I do, I had a knot in my stomach all day before her Wednesday morning coiling procedure. I knew that there was a possibility that the coiling would burst the aneurysm and she could die on the operating table. Tuesday afternoon was a rainy day in Portland, and I was on the east side of town making hospital visits. As I returned home in the late afternoon, I came over the hill and saw St. Vincent's Hospital to the right of Highway 26 in way I'd never seen it before.

The biggest, clearest rainbow I have ever seen stretched over St. Vincent's. It touched the earth on both sides and the colors were brilliant and amazing. I called Beth on my cell phone and said, "Beth, it's going to be okay. God put a rainbow over St. Vincent's, and you need to claim God's promise that God's going to be with you." People at St. Matthew know I get choked up about things like this, and Beth graciously heard my words amidst my tears.

Things did go well for Beth. Through her surgeries and chemotherapy she has continued her mass communication ministry by organizing our congregation's blood drives, calling lay readers, getting computer clickers for our worship services, initiating an e-mail prayer chain, and being on our Worship Ministry Team. She told me, "People will often ask me why I am doing this when I am 'sick,' and I explain that I need the human touch with those phone calls, and I cannot spend all day thinking about me and the fact that I have cancer. Life is much bigger than that, and it is such a gift for me to have these ministries." Beth knows that worship is a lifestyle and wishes to receive the wondrous gifts that God so graciously wants to give.

Paul and Silas

Think of Paul and Silas in prison. They were in deep trouble. They had been stripped, flogged, and clamped in prison stocks because of their commitment to Jesus. What would you have done? What would you do if you were imprisoned for your faith? What would you do if you (like Beth) were imprisoned in a body that was sentenced to cancer and possibly death?

Most of us would probably feel sorry for ourselves, and perhaps even give up. But that is not what Paul and Silas did. Instead, they worshiped God by singing praises to Jesus their Lord. They sang about Jesus, in spite of knowing what might happen to them. They offered songs of love as part of their commitment to being a living sacrifice to the God who created them and who loved them since the day of their inception.

They were saved not because of their worship or the style of their songs. We don't know whether they sang from an old hymnbook, made up new songs, chanted mantras, or sang multiple praise song choruses with varying intensity. What made the difference is the *one whom they loved.* The style of the songs they sang was immaterial; the focus of their songs made the difference in their lives.

Far too often churches focus more on the *how* of worship than on than on the One *whom* we worship. Lutherans are a more diverse group these days than they ever have been. Our worship styles are more diverse than they ever have been. Though we may prefer a particular style, it is important to remember that worship is not synonymous with music. Worship is not a particular liturgy. Worship is not the style of preaching. Worship is praising God as Giver of life, and worship is about receiving what God wants to give. Worship is not about us; it's about God. It's not a result of how well the music, preaching, ushering, or singing is done. It's not the result of whether I stand or sit or raise hands or kneel.

Worship is receiving what God wants to give. God is the primary actor in worship. And the style of worship is far less important than receiving what God wants to give. God wants to give us the forgiveness of sins, a restored and renewed life. God wants us to die to our sinful self and be raised to a new life. God wants Christ to live in us daily and have our lives reflect the light of Christ. God wants real worship for real life. Worship is a way that churches (and people) fulfill God's call on and in our lives. In worship we appropriate God's call and go forth as new creations. Worship is not about what we want; it's about receiving what God wishes to give.

Worship as response only happens when we reflect God's purpose in and through our lives. When we do that we can sing, "I love you, Lord," "Make me a servant," or "Lift high the cross, the love of God proclaim." God's purpose is that the world might know Jesus. The order of worship certainly helps us hear and experience God more fully, but the order itself is not the essence of worship.

Instead, God calls us through worship into the world to make disciples. In Jesus' last instruction to his disciples he said, "Go therefore and make disciples, baptizing them in the name of the Father and the Son and the Holy Spirit; teaching them to obey everything that I have commanded you, and lo, I am with you to the close of the age" (Matthew 28:16-20).

If we worship without heeding God's commission, or create worship services that alienate those whom God calls us to reach, are we really worshiping? If we focus on our needs, it's easy for the worship time to become a kind of social club experience. "I" liked this and not that. Pretty soon, we can begin to have either a critical attitude toward worship or appreciate the experience only when it suits our needs.

The only thing that matters is whether or not people who come to worship can receive what God wants to give. Worship wars in Lutheran congregations need to become a thing of the past; we're standing in the way of people knowing Jesus through which we discover God's purpose for our lives. It's critically important that we not stand in the way of that.

In my opinion, we don't want to lock ourselves into a church culture that asks everyone who comes to church to become like us. When someone comes to your new member class with more tattoos and body piercings than you have fingers and toes, we've missed the mark if we give the impression that being Lutheran in this place is mostly about coming to potlucks and bringing green gelatin with small marshmallows on top. What we need to do is provide worship that lifts up the gospel and challenges people to live as disciples of Christ, the One who has laid claim to their lives and who calls them to a life of purpose.

Think of worship as taking a shower. I dare say that many of us just love that warm morning shower as it gets us ready for the day. Like a warm inviting shower, worship can be a place to luxuriate, receiving bountiful blessings from God. But staying in the shower is not what life is about; you need to get out and share that bountiful blessing with others.

Most Lutherans love to stand in the shower, but we have difficulty taking on the rest of the day. We love to be showered with blessings on Sunday, but by Monday we're not ready to take those blessings of worship and bring them to those around us. We have a genetic predisposition to be *the frozen chosen,* but that certainly isn't biblical or faithful.

In touch with God's love

As we close this chapter, think of three ways to be in touch with God's love for your life. First, try to find some time each day to spend with God. It doesn't have to be long. It can be a simple regular routine at the beginning, middle, or end of the day when you just put everything aside and open your heart and mind to God. My personal routine is often to spend some time each morning in our hot tub (a West Coast "thing") where I just float in the warm waters, close my eyes, and ask God to be in my life that day and to give me direction. Jesus said, "But whenever you pray, go into your room, and shut the door and pray to the Father who is in secret; and your Father who sees in secret will reward you" (Matthew 6:6). I can't tell you the number of times that God has given me direction because of that morning time.

Second, develop a constant conversation with God. Psalm 105:4 says, "Seek the Lord and his strength; seek his presence continually." Some people shoot "arrow prayers" to God whenever they're at a stoplight or whenever they start their cars. Develop a consistent time for conversation with God. Others have "prayer dots," those sticky dots that they put on their mirror or on their watch or on the door going into their office. Whenever they see that "prayer dot" they simply say a three-sentence prayer. Others take time each day for "breathing prayer"—saying a word of thanks to God as they breath in and saying something they know they need to get out of their lives as they breathe out. Whatever method you use, develop a constant conversation with God.

Third, commit every day to doing something that draws you closer to God and God's love. Again, it's very important to remember that that there's absolutely nothing that you can do to make God love you more; God already loves you with an overwhelming love. There are things that you can do to help you love God more, and that can make a big difference in your life. As Rick Warren says, "It's not what you do that matters; it's who you do it for."[8]

This is not something we do alone. It is in fellowship with others that we experience and share the love of God. In the next chapter, we consider the importance of relationships within the body of Christ.

Questions for discussion

1. How would you describe the essence of worship? What brings you an experience with the presence of God?

2. What kind of worship style or styles does your church have? What worship style do you prefer? How can or does worship help you discover God's purpose for your life?

3. What is the most significant experience you've had in worship? What happened? What made the difference, and how did you feel?

4. Worship is described in the chapter as being in a shower. What other analogies would you use to describe worship?

3

Fellowship: The Purpose of Integration

Beloved, let us love one another; for anyone who loves God
is born of God and loves God.
Those who do not love do not know God, for God is love.
Beloved, let us love one another.
   —1 John 4:7-8

We can only be healthy human beings to the extent
that we invest time in building significant relationships
and connecting to supportive communities.[1]
   —Christine and Tom Sine

Blessed be the tie that binds, our hearts in Christian love;
The fellowship of kindred minds is like to that above.
   —John Fawcett, 1782

Individualism is increasingly becoming a part of our American culture. Far too many suburban home dwellers turn their homes into places of isolation. They come home from work, drive into the garage with their windows rolled up, and hardly even relate to their neighbors. Family rooms or great rooms with large screen TVs and multiple computers become a place of retreat. The communal front porch that existed for many of us in the days of our grandparents is virtually gone. The media emphasizes seeing ourselves as individual consumers, and malls become social gathering spaces as people shop until they drop.

One of the life purposes we need most but experience least is that of fellowship with other believers. We hardly experience fellowship outside of church; we sometimes have it even less at church. Paul writes in 2 Corinthians 8:5 that ". . . they gave themselves first to the Lord and, by the will of God, to us." They first gave themselves to God (worship) and then to us (fellowship). Fellowship is the second key to a purpose-filled life. Through fellowship we are not only believers, but "belongers." In Trinitarian language, we *believe* and trust in God, we *belong* to Jesus our Savior, and we *become* the body of Christ by the power of the Holy Spirit.

Paul encouraged Christian fellowship when he wrote: "Let love be genuine; hate what is evil, hold fast to what is good; love one another with mutual affection; outdo one another in showing honor. . . . Rejoice in hope, be patient in suffering, persevere in prayer. Contribute to the needs of the saints; extend hospitality to strangers" (Romans 12:10-13).

The need for Christian fellowship is in sharp contrast to the individualism and isolation that is prevalent in our culture. Jeff Whillock writes in his Doctor of Ministry Thesis:

> In spite of God's design in creation and destiny in redemption, our reality is that brokenness and sin are part of everyday life. It is, thus, crucial that people have a community where sinners can be forgiven, where the lonely can find a place to belong, where the lost can discern God's guidance, where the hurting and weeping can experience healing, and where the joyful can rejoice with others."[2]

Discipleship and "Grow" Groups

Jeff Whillock is a pastor at Bethlehem Lutheran Church in Aberdeen, South Dakota. Based on his experience in developing discipleship and fellowship groups at his previous church (St. John's Lutheran in Cedar Falls, Iowa), Jeff has developed a series of Grow Groups at Bethlehem Lutheran. Grow Groups are short-term (seven-week) groups centered around small group studies and discussions on the Sunday morning sermon. These Grow Groups are organized several times a year, because Whillock has found that short-term commitments tend to be more attractive to many people. However, many of the Grow Groups continue to meet after the seven weeks are over as participants discover the power of fellowship and grow through their experience together.

Jeff's thesis points to the connection between making disciples and life formation:

> In an effort to fulfill the great commission—"make disciples . . . teaching them"—some have sought to produce Christians who have been taught the right information. However, discipleship is not merely a matter of *information*, but, more holistically, a matter of *life-formation*. Jesus instructed the early followers to teach others "to obey." Obedience is not a matter of the intellect only; it involves one's whole life. The teaching intended by Jesus is cultivating relationships with the triune God through whom our lives are being transformed."[3]

The Grow Groups fit very well with Bethlehem's vision statement that includes the aspects of Welcoming, Worshiping, Teaching, and Serving. With a very easy structure, Grow Groups follow the *4 R Rhythm:*

• Reconnecting—a time for getting to know one another.

• Reading—a time for reading the Bible passage and sharing initial questions or insights.

• Reflecting—a time for allowing the passage to be a window into both the biblical world and our personal lives.

• Responding—a time for sharing how God may be leading you to respond in your relationships with God and with others.

The Grow Group experience has clearly impacted participants. One Bethlehem member shared his conviction that "if you want to know where God is in your life, join a Grow Group. If you don't believe in miracles, don't join a Grow Group!"

This kind of fellowship is easy to replicate at any Lutheran congregation. You don't need a new program that the pastor starts; you just have to do it. Gather some friends from church or from your neighborhood. You don't need permission to start a group like this; just do it.

Jim is a member of Bethlehem Lutheran in Aberdeen, and works at Student Loan Finance Corporation. He grew up Methodist and experienced his early days in a strict, critical church. He didn't go to church in college, but after he got married and started a family, Jim and his wife both felt the need to join a congregation. Upon the recommendation of a friend, they started church shopping, went to Bethlehem, and decided it was going to be their church home.

Shortly after they joined Bethlehem, Al Schnoover became senior pastor, and the church's mission changed to more of a youth and family emphasis. That drew Jim and his family in even more deeply.

But what has been personally life transforming for Jim has been his involvement in a Men's Grow Group, led by Pastor Jeff. Jim, Jeff, and a group of other men meet every other week at church during the lunch hour. They talk about their life, their faith, and their struggles. They read the Sunday morning lessons and reflect on what it means for their lives. They share deeply about what it means to be a man of faith and how they can raise their children with biblical values. Every time they meet God is present with this group of men who seek God's purpose and direction for their lives. Together they share, struggle, pray—and grow—in faith.

It has changed the way Jim looks at life in his job, and at the way he sees others at home, church, and work. Jim told me that he grew up hearing sermons about not drinking and dancing, but now he hears sermons about reaching out to those whose lives are hurt and shattered. He said, "I look at things differently; I don't look at how people might annoy me, but I look at how I might be of service to them. Service isn't just something you do; it's something you receive as a gift from God."

Jim's Grow Group is not just a support group where people talk about their problems. Instead, it is focused on how following Christ can affect all one does. Pastor Jeff continually reminds them that there's a great power and purpose for their lives, and that the group is not there to commiserate about their problems, but to consecrate their futures.

Jim found he really needed the Group and the vision he received there, especially as the past year has been difficult for him. His aunt (who he considers his grandmother) died last January, his father died in April, and recently his brother was diagnosed with cancer. Jim's Grow Group was a new experience for him, and he appreciated having older men who offered him their experience. One is a leukemia survivor, and another is a liver transplant survivor who supported him as he grieved his brother's cancer. They know what he's going through as a fellowship of sufferers. Since Jim's family is so spread out across the United States, they mostly communicate through phone calls, but Jim has found that a congregational fellowship group has supported him through difficult times. There's someone who knows his name and his struggles, and that makes all the difference in the world.

Trinity groups

Trinity Lutheran Church is in the northern panhandle of Idaho. Bonners Ferry is the last real town before the Canadian Border. Alison is the church secretary there and has also been a part of the Evangelism Team. Several people on that team were inspired by reading *The Purpose-Driven Life* and decided to work with the pastor on doing a 40 Days of Purpose campaign. Through the campaign they had thirteen small groups with a total of about 85 people—not bad for a congregation that averages 120 in worship in a town of 2,400 people!

Because of the fellowship groups, the church became an even friendlier place. They started using nametags on Sunday morning, developed a deeper sense of commitment to one another, and intensified their spiritual experience. The Parish Education Committee started offering different kinds of classes more related to living out your faith, and people began to volunteer for ministry more enthusiastically.

The church used Kelly Fryer's *No Experience Necessary* in their young adult class. The study reached them at their level, and one young man who participated was brought back into active involvement and off the inactive list.

Alison said, "It's kind of like a whole group of people who go to the same movie, and even though they didn't know one another before, they have shared a common experience. It's been good for us."

Life together

Fellowship doesn't just mean coming to church and having a cup of coffee and chatting about the town's football game. It's sharing life together. Many Lutheran churches settle for such conversation as their primary form of fellowship, but it's much more than that. It's also important to point out that fellowship does not necessarily happen just through constant involvement in your church's programs.

Everything we've been talking about so far is not about starting to attend another church program. Often, we're far too programmed already in everything we do. The last thing I want to do is to add another church program onto what you're already doing.

I would like to direct the focus of your fellowship to a more fulfilling expression. You see, much of what Lutheran churches have done is to work toward fellowship in all the wrong places. We've been drawn into the success mode of program-driven churches that tell us that we need to offer more and more programs to meet the needs of a consumerist clientele and society. We've been told that the needs of the individual are more important than the needs of the community, and so we spin our wheels by trying to create programs and opportunities that we think people want and which will encourage them to become members of our congregations.

When we transfer this consumer culture to the programs of our church, we get fellowship wrong. Christian fellowship is not about affirming the middle class values of life. Church is not the place where we go to get our needs met. For far too many years of my ministry I tried to offer programs that competed with the local YMCA, the local health club, the various schools, and secular clubs like Rotary and Kiwanis. Christian fellowship is not a program; it's a way of life.

The biblical model of the church is an incarnational, relational community. Jesus prayed, "Sanctify them in truth; your word is truth. As you have sent me into the world, so I have sent them into the world" (John 17:17-18). The biblical model of the church is to incarnate the presence of Jesus (to be sanctified) and to be sent into the world. It is through fellowship within the church that we realize that it is only God's Word, incarnated through other believers, that can reveal our sin to us, motivate us to acknowledge that sin and to repent, and to direct us to a life of transformation. This is not something we can do on our own. In Luther's explanation to the Third Article of the Apostles' Creed he writes:

> I believe that I cannot by my own reason or strength believe in Jesus Christ, my Lord, or come to him. But the Holy Spirit has called me though the Gospel, enlightened me with his

gifts, and sanctified and preserved me in the true faith, just as he calls, gathers, enlightens and sanctifies the whole Christian church on earth, and preserves it in union with Jesus Christ in the one true faith.[4]

Fellowship is a sanctified community. A reinvented church would be more relational and less institutional. It would focus more on the needs of those outside the building than those inside the building. It would be more focused on being conformed to the image of Christ than on having our consumer needs met. It would be an incarnational community that is made and kept holy.

In the 40 Days of Purpose Campaign, Rick Warren identifies four levels of fellowship. The first level of fellowship is membership, choosing to belong. Membership is making a choice about being a part of a church family and becoming connected to the body of Christ. The Christian faith is not a matter of just believing, but it's also a matter of belonging. It's at church where you get to live out what it means to be a child of God and where each member belongs to and supports all the others (Romans 12:5).

The next level is friendship, learning to share. Friendship is built by participating in a group where we can share both our struggles and our joys. The Christian life is not a solo act; there are no Lone Ranger Christians. Learning to share our experiences, our challenges, and our daily walk is an essential part of fellowship.

The third level of fellowship is partnership, doing my part. Partnership means that you have a contribution to make to the family of God. God did not create you to be a consumer; God created you to give back to the family of God and to make a difference in the world. Partnership means finding a ministry in the church and a mission in the world.

The fourth level of fellowship is kinship, loving believers like family. The second chapter of Acts describes the early believers as family, and they shared all they had in common. It's this level that

Jesus was talking about when he said that whoever does the will of God is his mother, brother, and sister. When you know that and experience it, it changes your life.

Which level of fellowship do you currently experience? Are you a member of a church, but don't have many friends there? Do you have friends at church but don't feel a real partnership with them in ministry? At whatever level you currently experience fellowship, take action to draw yourself deeper into fellowship at your church. Talk to others or talk to your pastor and find ways in which you can make this happen. If you do, you will discover yourself living closer to your life purpose.

You were put on this earth for a loving relationship with God and with others. You weren't put on this earth to lead a life of materialism or to only be concerned about your own pleasure or success. When I'm with people in the hospital who are dying, I've never heard anyone in their dying moments ask for their diplomas, or for their sporting trophies, or even for their PDA. When they reach those final moments in life they know that all that matters is knowing Jesus and being surrounded by loving family and friends. You were formed to be a part of God's family and to live in fellowship with other believers.

Questions for discussion

1. Where is Christian fellowship most fulfilling in your life? Do you have a group of Christian friends with whom you share your joys and sorrows?

2. Do you identify with the increasing isolation in our culture? How do you see today's isolation compared to ten years ago? Five years ago? What are three factors that have contributed to the isolation?

3. What is your reaction to the idea that Christian faith is about belonging, as much as believing?

4. What can you do in the next month to strengthen your fellowship with other believers?

4

Discipleship: The Passion to Become Like Christ

For those whom he foreknew he also predestined to be conformed to the image of his son in order that he might be the firstborn within a large family.
—Romans 8:29

We must no longer be children . . .
But speaking the truth in love we must grow up in every way into him who is the head, into Christ . . .
—Ephesians 4:14-15

I remember the day my first son, Matthew, was born. As I spent time with him those first hours of his life I was just amazed at how beautifully he was created. I gazed at his fingers, stroked his ears, and was profoundly thankful for the gift he was. As I spent time with him during the next months I loved everything about him—his smile, his sounds, and yes, even his cries and his diapers.

I loved him at every stage: as a baby, as a two-year-old toddler, as an attentive first grader, as a fun middle schooler, as an active high school student, and now as a young man in his junior year at Pacific Lutheran University. I loved him as a baby, but I'm sure glad he didn't stay that way.

Part of the natural process of life is to grow, mature, learn, and experience many different things. In Ephesians 4:15-16 we read, "But speaking the truth in love, we must *grow up in every way* into him who is the head, into Christ, from whom the whole body, joined and knit together by every ligament with which it is equipped, as each part is working properly, promotes the body's growth in *building itself up* in love" (emphasis mine). Growing in discipleship is the third purpose for your life.

One of Rick Warren's convictions is that it is in discipleship that we find we were created to become like Christ. That may be offensive to some Lutherans. How can we possibly become like Christ? It's absolutely clear that we can't be Christ, nor will we ever even be close to being anything remotely like God. Adam and Eve discovered that. They were tempted to become like God and to gain special knowledge of good and evil, knowledge reserved for God alone. Their overreaching was the sin that caused them to be sent out of the Garden of Eden.

On the other hand, think of the following Bible passages (the emphasis is mine):

"For those whom he foreknew he also predestined *to be conformed to the image of his Son.*" (Romans 8:29)

"And all of us . . . are being *transformed into the same image* from one degree of glory to another; for this comes from the Lord, the Spirit." (2 Corinthians 3:18)

"Just as we have borne the image of the man of dust, we will also bear *the image of the man of heaven.*" (1 Corinthians 15:49)

In the *Lutheran Book of Worship (LBW)* we say these words: "Almighty God, you gave your Son both as a sacrifice for sin and a *model of the godly life.* Enable us to receive him always with thanksgiving, and to *conform our lives to his;* through the same Jesus Christ our Lord."[1]

The new *Evangelical Lutheran Worship* resource contains the words: "God of all mercy and consolation, come to the aid of your people, turning us from our sin to live for you alone. Give us the power of your Holy Spirit that we may confess our sins, receive your forgiveness, and *grow into the fullness of your Son,* Jesus Christ our Lord."[2]

You can't do it alone. But then again, it's not about you. It's about God and God's purpose for your life. What might the Holy Spirit do in you?

The trilogy of thinking, feeling, and acting

Living according to God's purpose involves a trilogy of thinking, feeling, and acting. This trilogy can also refer to the mind, will, and conduct or to convictions, character, and conduct. They all have to do with the head, heart, and hands. All three need to be engaged. Living according to God's purpose means you need to grow into discipleship in such a way that you enlighten your mind, engage your emotions, and challenge your will. Think of it this way:

- Enlighten your mind so that you can think like Jesus in your convictions (head).
- Engage your emotions so that you can feel like Jesus in your character (heart).
- Challenge your will so that you can act like Jesus in your conduct (hands).[3]

Growth in discipleship needs to be varied, but it needs to be constant. If you're not growing, you're dying, both physically and spiritually. Part of the challenge in the Lutheran church is that many people stop growing after confirmation, and many people quit going to church (or take a break) after high school. That means that their spiritual development levels off or shuts down altogether. The problem is that the struggles and challenges of life grow pretty exponentially after high school. If there hasn't been spiritual development happening all along then it leaves us unprepared for the moral complexities of life that confront us in our later years. Since you can't resolve graduate school problems with a middle school education, it leaves many people totally ill-equipped for following Jesus with their convictions, character, and conduct. It takes a lifetime to develop being like Christ in your head, heart, and hands, but that's the goal that God has for each and every one of us.

Lillian's life lessons

Our Saviour's Lutheran Church in Naperville, Illinois, is a very large congregation where Tom Grevlos serves as senior pastor. Tom has always been an advocate of learning and discipleship and was excited about the growth of discipleship opportunities when Our Saviour's entered into a 40 Days of Purpose campaign. Tom told me the following:

> The experience of 40 Days at Our Saviour's in the fall of 2004 was exceptional. Counting men, women, and children, there were over one thousand people involved in the six-week emphasis on a regular basis. We had people walk in off the street after seeing our banner, and a number of new families joined the congregation and have stayed quite active. Our small group ministry groups doubled from twenty-five to fifty groups, with some even working through the book a second time, without the videotapes. The success of the organized effort has also launched a stronger Adult Growth emphasis, including Sunday night mini-courses for blocks of time called "Sunday Night Soul Food." We hosted a LifeKeys conference in January and are using that as a follow-up for gift identification and discovery. This fall we are launching a similar campaign but using the Alpha Series Course, with over one hundred who have already gone through Alpha serving as our planning teams.

Though very few Lutheran congregations can match the numbers or the activity that Tom talks about, it's all about changing lives one at a time.

One whose life was changed was Lillian, a member at Our Saviour's. Lillian is in her early seventies and has a marvelous attitude and spirit. She lives with her sister who is wheelchair bound. Lillian has a heart for the Lord, and the 40 Days of Purpose campaign was just what she needed to focus on changing lives through discipleship. She was a small group leader of twelve women who regularly attended the weekly small groups. She is a self-confessed non-teacher, but she relied on the Holy Spirit to speak to her and to her small group about what they were to do.

Lillian is a master at hospitality. She provided coffee and donuts at each session, welcomed people to the group, organized everything so it would be easy for all participants, and made everyone feel welcomed and valued. Each week they used the Lutheran discussion guide provided at www.purposedrivenlutherans.com and talked about their lives, and not just the material from the 40 Days resource. Lillian said, "It was so wonderful; it was the most wonderful thing I've ever done!"

After they went through the entire study they wanted to keep going, so now they're reading and discussing one day of the book each week. Each week Lillian writes a study curriculum built around each chapter. She reads through the book and shortens each chapter/day, and writes down the things she thinks is important. She branched out to ask her small group members to think about what it really means to be Lutheran and immersed herself in the Bible, the Small Catechism, the writings of Dietrich Bonhoeffer, and other people's experiences.

Lillian wants people to discover what their lives are about, and not simply to be told. Knowing more about Jesus and acting accordingly needs to come from people's hearts. Lillian said that each time they met the group prayed for the Holy Spirit to be with them in their discussions and in their consequent commitments. At a celebration banquet at the church Lillian, who told me that love for Jesus always characterized her group, said, "The reason for our success as a group is the love for each other. If we go in with love, not for ourselves, but for spreading the word and helping each other, we can't fail. It's not about us, it's about God."

Pastor Tom Grevlos said, "Lillian's mantra is that God isn't finished with me yet!" That's pretty good evidence that a life with Christ is always growing and developing!

Nurturing faith at home

Discipleship begins with relationship. Learning new information is important, but being in relationship with God and with others is critical to growing faith. But it's not automatic. In families, for example, discipleship is learned not just by listening but by observing. The family system provides the greatest opportunities for growth in faith. Think of that and the importance for our Lutheran congregations.

When I was a young (and naive) pastor I thought that my role was to take children and confirmation-aged students and educate them about the Christian faith. Parents, I thought, were just fine, but it was the primary role of the pastor to teach the young about the Christian faith.

How wrong I was.

Without a household of faith, whatever I did was almost a waste of time. The church is not the primary laboratory for discipleship training—the home is. Without parents and aunts and uncles who model and teach the Christian faith, discipleship simply falls short. It's trite to say that it takes a village to raise a child, but it's true to say that children who are not raised by parents who provide a faith-based home life, probably aren't strong candidates for Christian faith, let alone discipleship.

At St. Matthew we've totally adopted the family ministry philosophy from the Youth and Family Institute. It is spelled out in a book called *Frogs Without Legs Can't Hear: Nurturing Disciples in Home and Congregation*[4] by David W. Anderson and Paul Hill. We became convinced that the church cannot provide training in discipleship without being in partnership with the home. In the book, David and Paul write:

> A healthy environment for faith formation is more complex than what takes place within the congregational walls, however. The faith life of the home is also critical. The term *home* for us is not merely the place where one lives and the people who live there. Rather, home is the larger network of relationships and daily life experience of people of faith. Home is a metaphorical image to describe the intersection of faith and daily life.[5]

The church always needs to be asking the discipleship question: "How are we forming faith?" This model of discipleship is based on five principles and four keys. Let me briefly summarize each one.

Five principles

The first principle is that *faith is formed through personal, trusted relationships*. Mothers and fathers influence faith more than anyone else ever will. Parents play the primary role of developing followers of Jesus. Therefore, the role of the church is to develop the faith lives of parents who can teach their children what it means to believe and follow Jesus.

The second principle is that *the church is a living partnership between home and congregation*. The role of the church is not to provide a multitude of programs that just keep us busier. Instead, the role of the church is to strengthen the bonds between the congregation and the faith laboratory of the home. The church needs to provide resources where parents can support and encourage their children, nurture them in the way in which they spend their time and money, pray for them as they grow and mature, and worship with them on a regular basis.

The third principle is that *home is church, too.* As a church we need to see ourselves as supporters of what happens at home, sometimes even in the car on the way home from church. We shouldn't be asking how we can get more people in worship; we need to be asking how we can help parents be faith evangelists in their own homes. Just as Martin Luther provided the Small Catechism for parents to teach their children about the faith, so we need to claim that heritage and provide resources for parents to help their children follow Jesus more closely and clearly.

The fourth principle is that *faith is more caught than taught.* Parents need to realize that they are the Christian curriculum that their children see! Our children watch us every day, and our actions speak louder than our words.

The fifth principle is that *it takes Christian parents and other adults to raise Christian youth.* Parents simply cannot delegate the faith formation of their children to the youth pastor or to other teachers. Already the media drives a wedge between generations; it's the church's role to bridge that gap and provide Christian parents, aunts, uncles, baptismal sponsors, and everyone in the congregation to commit to raising Christian youth.

Four keys

Besides those five principles there are four keys that help congregations provide resources for families. At St. Matthew we've totally reoriented our Sunday preaching and Sunday school teaching around these principles, and are providing on-line and printed materials so that the Sunday morning sermons align with what children are taught in Sunday school. Making sure everyone is being taught the same lesson has revolutionized our life together. Parents are provided a variety of resources that they can use to "disciple" their children.

The first key is *caring conversations*. It's a way that parents and children can practice the presence of God. Sharing one's faith, values, and stories through caring conversations is key for children to make the important link between faith and life.

The second key is *devotions*. Since what they were taught in Sunday school is also the theme of Sunday morning worship, it's much easier to have families immersed in the same theme or Bible verse. Everything is aligned according to the same theme or message.

The third key is *service*. We all know that service to others transforms the way in which we live our lives. When families are engaged in service together, they discover more meaning, and they grow in faith together.

The fourth key is *rituals and traditions*. Rituals are patterns that occur regularly and communicate meaning, values, and faith. For a much fuller explanation with resources go to www.youthandfamily-institute.org or www.alifeworthleading.org.

Once you realize that you were created for a relationship with God and God's family, then discipleship (becoming like Christ) becomes a primary goal of your life. Remember that God does God's part in "working in" us for our salvation while we "work out" the implications of discipleship for our lives.

A family discipleship model

Bethlehem Lutheran in Aberdeen, South Dakota, (described in the previous chapter) has fully implemented the family discipleship model described above. Scott is a father of a thirteen-year-old and nine year-old and has been a member of Bethlehem for the past fourteen years. He really appreciates what the church's Faith Milestones emphasis has done for his family. The first significant Faith Milestone was a "prayer pillow" made by the women of the church. The pillow contains a pocket where parents or pastors can put in written prayer cards for their children to sleep on. His daughter got a pillow when she was three years old, so the pillow is now flat and the pouch is worn, but she still insists on sleeping with it, even when they are camping! When his daughter was four years old she was presented with a Beginner's Bible, fifty chapters of wonderful Bible stories that he's read several times through with each child.

Each year something different is given during worship for each age group. Fifth graders are given flashlights and told to let their lights so shine. It may not seem like much to older members of the congregation, but Scott's daughter sure got the point!

In sixth grade they're given a locker mirror to attach to their lockers at school with the words *Imago Dei* ("In the image of God"). When friends ask what it means, it's wonderful for an eleven year-old to give a witness of faith. When students are sixteen they have a "Blessing of the Keys" ceremony on Sunday morning, when parents and kids come forward, put the car keys in the baptismal font, bless them, and ask for God to watch over them as they drive alone.

Al Schnoover, the senior pastor at Bethlehem has been responsible for the transformation of an aging Lutheran congregation to one that's brought in nine hundred new members over the past six years, mostly because of the congregation's passion for discipleship and for emphasizing the role of home and family in nurturing disciples.

These are just a few examples of how congregations and individuals are finding purpose in making disciples. Disciples are active and engaged in the life of faith. Congregations that emphasize and encourage this kind of discipleship will see more people committed to following Jesus, and living with a greater sense of purpose.

In the next chapter we'll talk about living out your discipleship in a life of ministry. Ministry is not just something the pastor does; it's far more important than that!

Questions for discussion

1. In what primary way(s) do you express your faith? Is it with your head, heart, or hands? What have you done in the past month to express your faith?

2. What are some of the practices of faith in your home? What special rituals or traditions do you have with your family? What can you do to make your home a faith laboratory for those who live there?

3. What did you think about the five principles and the four keys? What did you find most captivating?

5

Ministry: The Process of Involvement

Purpose is the place where your deep gladness meets the world's needs.
—Frederick Buechner

Living for Jesus a life that is true,
Striving to please him in all that I do;
Yielding allegiance, glad-hearted and free,
This is the pathway of blessing for me.[1]
—Thomas O. Chisholm

When I played high school football, I always hated sitting on the bench. The problem was, I did it a lot.

During my junior year I spent ten weeks as a punching bag for the senior line, made up of a group of guys who were all 6'4" and 240 pounds. I always hoped that I would be put in even during the final two minutes when we were ahead (or behind) 42-7, but the coach didn't think we juniors were either talented or tough enough, so we didn't get out on the field once all year. My senior year was much more rewarding; I played both offense and defense each and every game and was on the field of play every moment of every game. It was glorious.

Some people live their lives on the bench. They know there's a game going on, but they watch from a distance and don't get on the field of play. It's not because a coach won't put them in; it's because they either don't want to play the game, or they just don't know the rules of the game.

Ministry with purpose

Ministry is the fourth way to discover the purpose of your life. It's the second part of Jesus' commandment to love: loving God is worship and loving others is ministry. But how do you do it? Where do you start?

As you've read through this book you've seen the importance of starting with God. Take a moment away from reading, and write down five of the most important gifts God has given you. Then write down five things in your life that you've done that you feel best about, five experiences or accomplishments from which you draw the most satisfaction.

After you've done that, take some time thinking about the following questions. Consider reading the questions, and then taking a break while you think about them. Take a fifteen-minute walk around the block. Sit in the hot tub (that's what I do!). Take a break in your favorite chair where you can have some uninterrupted time. Think about how you would answer these questions:

- What do I care about most? Where am I most passionate?
- What are the biggest concerns in my life? What needs changing, and how can I assist in that change?
- When I daydream about making a difference in life, what is it I dream about?
- If I could leave my mark on any area of life, what would it be?
- How am I making a difference in the world?
- What is the legacy I wish to leave with my life?

As you think about those questions I hope you've thought both about what you might do, and where you might need to do it. The "what" has to do with your gifts and abilities; the "where" has to do with your passions and desires. Your gifts, abilities, passions, and desires are all given to you by God, and as you live into them you discover God's purpose for you.

You honor God by being true to the way God has created you. By using your gifts, abilities, passions, and desires to make a difference in the world, you are answering God's call on your life. And remember, "whatever you do in word or deed, do everything in the name of the Lord Jesus, giving thanks to God through him" (Colossians 2:6; 3:17).

When I was in grade school I wasn't always well-behaved. And every once in a while, when I was sentenced to a time-out in the hall, the teacher would come out and say to me, "Burtness, when you were made, God broke the mold."

The teacher meant it as an insult. But it's exactly true. There's never been, nor will there ever be, anyone like you with your gifts, abilities, passions, or desires. You are absolutely unique. God broke your mold. Think of these words from Psalm 139:

> O Lord, you have searched me and known me.
> You know when I sit down and when I rise up;
> you discern my thoughts from far away.
> Even before a word is on my tongue,
> O Lord, you know it completely.
> For it was you who formed my inward parts;
> you knit me together in my mother's womb.
> I praise you, for I am fearfully and wonderfully made.
> Wonderful are your works;
> that I know very well. (139:1-2, 4, 13-14)

God loves us and has a place where you are uniquely gifted for ministry. When you open yourself to what God might want to do with your life you'll discover a deep sense of meaning and significance. There is a place and a time that God has created for you. As we think about that, let's consider a Bible story.

The story of Esther

The book of Esther is a wonderful story of how Esther helped to save her Jewish people. She was a beautiful young Jewish woman who became the Queen of Persia and lived in the Persian Empire when Xerxes was the King of Persia. The events in the story took place around the time that Ezra rebuilt the new temple in Jerusalem, and Nehemiah rebuilt the walls of Jerusalem between 450 and 425 B.C. There are four key characters in the book of Esther:

Xerxes: The indulgent and indifferent Persian King

Mordecai: The shrewd mentor (and uncle) of Esther

Esther: The beautiful Jewish heroine who became Xerxes' queen

Haman: The vain and vicious villain

Young King Xerxes inherited the powerful Persian throne from his father, and as one who stumbled into wealth and fortune and status, he lived an indulgent lifestyle. He loved parties, friends, and beautiful women. Apparently not particularly bright, Xerxes could be easily manipulated.

Shortly after he became king, Xerxes threw a party for some very influential people that lasted seven days. In the middle of the party and he asked his wife, Queen Vashti, to come out and show all of the people how beautiful she was. She realized she was being asked to parade herself and be gawked at, so she refused. That made King Xerxes furious. He thought that if she disgraced the king in such a public matter, then no man in his empire would be safe from future disgrace at the hands of the wives. For her refusal to appear before the guests, Xerxes banished Vashti from the Empire.

Not being the sharpest tool in the shed, Xerxes quickly realized that he now did not have a queen to take care of him. Some friends convinced him to have a beauty pageant to find the most beautiful single woman in the Empire. Enter Esther, a young Jewish woman who had been orphaned but raised as a daughter by her kind Uncle Mordecai. Esther and Mordecai were among the Jewish people who had been living in captivity in Babylon before Babylon fell to the Persians. Mordecai encouraged Esther to enter into the beauty pageant but not to tell anyone that she was Jewish.

Esther won the pageant and became the new Queen of Persia. Haman, the vain and vicious villain, was one of the highest ranking officials in Persia, and he convinced King Xerxes to make every-one bow down before him as he walked through town. Everyone did, except Mordecai. Mordecai was a faithful Jew, who believed it was wrong to bow or pay homage to anyone but God. It bothered Haman to no end when he walked through town and everyone bowed down to him except Mordecai.

When Haman discovered that Mordecai was Jewish, he con-vinced King Xerxes to have all the Jews in the area killed. Xerxes agreed that the Jews were a great political threat to Persia. After Haman contributed a large amount of money to the King's treasury, he decreed that all the Jews should be killed.

When Mordecai heard of this, he sent word to Queen Esther that she must go to the king right away and plead the case for the Jewish people. At first, Esther resisted. She knew that if she walked in on the king without permission she could be banished from the kingdom. She would lose her place of prominence and promise.

The first lesson we learn from Esther is that life is never without struggles, even for people of faith. Even though Esther was one of God's chosen people, and she was beautiful and privileged, she stood to lose everything by going to Xerxes. Being a believer in God and a follower of Christ does not mean that we live in a protective bubble that keeps us from harm and evil. No matter how strongly we believe in God, tragedies and difficulties such as crime, divorce, unexpected death, and dread diseases will invade our homes. Even Jesus promised trouble when he spoke with his disciples (John 16:33). There are no places to hide or escape from the struggles of life.

Even so, in the midst of struggles and challenges God promises to be present with us. Jesus said that we would face troubles, but he also said that where I am, there you may also be (John 14:3). In Psalm 23, the psalmist promises that those who walk through the valley of the shadow of death will have no fear of evil because God is with them, protecting them with a rod and staff.

Where have you had trouble in life? Where have you had difficulties? What are the deep hurts that you carry with you? Places of challenge and difficulty are prime times to discover your purpose. God never wastes a hurt. People who have been through trouble in life are often gifted to minister to others who are experiencing that same trouble.

Esther considered what she should do. She knew that if she were to go to the king on behalf of her people, she might lose her comfort and status. It would have been easy for her to remain safe, to think that someone else should do it or that it just wasn't her responsibility.

Sometimes counting the cost of following God's call is simply too much. Some people see the price tag, the risk, and the inconvenience, and they think that the cost of following God's call is simply too much. They don't risk. They don't sacrifice. They'd rather live a safe, successful life than live a sacrificial, significant life. They'd rather protect their lives than really live their lives. Do you know people who just remain in dead-end jobs that make them miserable because they're afraid to take the risk of leaving? Do you know people who resist drawing close to other people because they don't want to take the risk of getting hurt? If it's true that purpose is often discovered in the place where your gladness meets the world's needs, then we need to be prepared to respond.

Just such a time as this

Mordecai responded to Esther's reluctance by saying, "Who knows? Perhaps you have come to royal dignity for just such a time as this."

Perhaps you have come to this point in your life for just such a time as this. Have you ever thought that the whole drama of your life will depend on your response to God's call? Have you ever wondered whether the whole meaning of your life is sometimes determined by how you respond to a single moment? Have you ever had the experience that there is at least one moment in life that makes sense of all the other moments, and you know why you are here and what you have to do? That was this moment for Esther.

The message of the book of Esther is that at a particular moment God called a young Jewish girl to save God's holy people from certain death at the hands of Xerxes and Haman. God placed Esther at that specific place for a strategic ministry purpose. Five hundred years later God would call another young Jewish girl at a specific place for strategic ministry purpose in order to save God's holy people—including you and me—from certain death. This time her name would be Mary and her son, Jesus, would become the Savior of the world.

God continues to place people at specific places for strategic ministry purposes. Perhaps God has a specific place for you at your school, your office, your neighborhood, or even in your family. Perhaps the strategic ministry purpose God has for you has not yet been made clear to you. I believe that there will be a time when you find yourself in an Esther-like situation, and you will discover why you are where you are and for what task or reason you are being called.

Moving on after moving in

Julie was called at a time such as this. She and her husband lived in Naperville, Illinois, and they enjoyed their life there until her husband was transferred to the East Coast. The move was difficult for Julie. She was apart from her friends and family and any other support group. Nobody knew her and, with small children, she didn't have a lot of adult contact. She became frustrated and depressed and wondered what she was supposed to do with her life.

Within a year her husband was offered another job back in Naperville, and he accepted. When they moved back to Naperville, they were looking for a church to join. They drove by Our Saviour's Lutheran in Naperville, Illinois (mentioned in chapter 4), which was just starting a 40 Days of Purpose Campaign and had all the signs and banners. It was just what Julie needed, so she took the risk and signed up for a women's small group.

She enjoyed the experience very much, and she started praying about other ways she could be involved at the church. Julie had been involved in previous women's Bible studies in other churches, but she did not really find them fulfilling. At Our Saviour's things were different. She enjoyed meeting and sharing with the women, and it lit a fire under her.

One Sunday morning Jeannie Grevlos, the senior pastor's wife, asked Julie if she'd be interested in a "move in" ministry. Jeannie knew the difficulty Julie had with her move to the east coast, and that there are many people who have struggles in relocating. She also knew about Julie's background in real estate. Since Naperville has a large group of people in transition, many need to talk about and deal with the issues of relocation.

Because of what Julie had recently experienced, she felt she was called just for a time like this. With a ready-made curriculum from Susan Miller's *After the Boxes Are Unpacked: Moving on After Moving In* and the support of the leadership of the church, Julie has started a ministry team for women who are struggling with relocation.

God placed Julie in a specific place for a specific calling, even though it came through difficult times. She's learned the difference between clinging and cherishing. You don't cling to the memories after relocation, but instead you cherish them and then move on. Her painful experience with relocation has helped her bless other women and become a powerful ministry.

No turning back

Let's return to Esther and realize the enormity of the task before her. She knew her success was not guaranteed. She knew that it might even cost her life, and she realized that she could not face it alone. She asked the Jews in the region to be in prayer for her (Esther 4:15-16), asking them to fast, think, and pray on her behalf. She totally committed herself to her ministry purpose and said, "And if I perish, I perish." Esther did what God wanted her to do. She opened her heart to a ministry concern, she deliberated and counted the cost, and she allowed her life to be challenged.

Perhaps you already know what kind of ministry God has called you to do. Perhaps you are struggling or deliberating or counting the cost. Perhaps you are waiting to discover God's ministry purpose for you. Just remember that the whole course of your life will be determined by how you follow God's call and purpose for your life.

Consider praying this prayer right now:

Lord Jesus, I live in a needy world. I believe you have put me where I am for a reason and a purpose. Loving Lord, guide me and lead me to a place that will challenge me to express the purpose in life that you have for me. Encourage me to make a commitment and to live my life for your kingdom. In Jesus' name. Amen.

A letter to yourself

Consider this exercise. Pretend it is your seventieth birthday. You are preparing to write a letter to a loved one, looking back over your life and telling your loved one what was important about the way you lived your life and the way you gave of yourself. In what way have you given of your time, talents, and treasures that provide you with the most satisfaction? How have you used the time that God has given you to help make life better for someone less fortunate? How have you made Jesus first in your life? What are your particular God-given gifts, abilities, passions, and desires? How can God use them in ministry? What's your legacy? Is it what you have accumulated in your garage and attic? Is it the trophies, the diplomas, and the titles you had? Or is it a life of loving God and others?

When you've answered these questions, consider how you can put your sense of calling to work. How can you lose yourself in service to God and others? Life consists of action verbs. It is through action that you will have discovered the true meaning of the purpose of ministry.

Robert Driver-Bishop writes about the familiar story of the Good Samaritan, and he writes about the "action verbs" in the story: "The Samaritan acted out of love and compassion: 'He *went* to him and *bandaged* his wounds, and *poured* oil and wine on them. Then he *put* him on his own animal, *brought* him to an inn, and *took care* of him.' The next day he followed with further action by *giving* the landlord two silver pieces (enough for a week's lodging) and *guaranteed* payment of further expenses."[2]

John Ortberg has a great book titled, *If You Want to Walk on Water, You've Got to Get out of the Boat.*[3]

It's time to get out of the boat.

Questions for discussion

1. What would your life look like if you spent two hours each week in active service or witness in your community? Where would you spend that time? What would it take to get you started?

2. Read Psalm 139. What images of God come to mind? What words describe how God feels about you?

3. What does this verse mean to you: *Living for Jesus, wherever I am, doing each duty in his holy name; willing to suffer affliction and loss, deeming each trial a part of my cross.* How does it relate to discovering your life purpose?

6

Evangelism: The Importance of Inviting

Go therefore and make disciples of all nations.
  —Matthew 28:20

I love to tell the story of unseen things above,
Of Jesus and his glory, of Jesus and his love.
I love to tell the story, because I know 'tis true
It satisfies my longings as nothing else can do

I love to tell the story! 'Twill be my theme in glory
To tell the old, old story of Jesus and His love.
  —Katherine Hankey

Two of my favorite Bible verses talk specifically about the purpose that God has for our lives. One is from Jeremiah 29:11, 13-14: "For surely I know the plans I have for you, says the LORD, plans for your welfare and not for harm, to give you a future with hope. When you search for me, you will find me; if you seek me with all your heart, I will let you find me, says the LORD."

The other is Jesus' words in John 17:4, in which he prays to God: "I glorified you on earth by finishing the work that you gave me to do."

These verses talk about purpose, vision, significance, and direction for life. God has plans for us, and God has promised that we will find God's purpose if we are open to searching for it. Jesus knew that God had given him a life purpose, and he completed the purpose for which God sent him into the world.

So far in this book we've seen these four purposes for our lives:

• Worship means that we were planned for God's pleasure.
• Fellowship means that we were formed for God's family.
• Discipleship means that we were created to become like Christ.
• Ministry means that we were shaped for serving God.

The fifth purpose for your life is based on the God's call to practice evangelism—you were made for a mission.[1] God has a purpose for your life. God wants you to fulfill that purpose before you die. The purpose has to do with sharing God's love with others. You were made for a mission to share Christ.

That kind of sharing doesn't come naturally for Lutherans. Perhaps you've heard the old joke about what you get when you cross a Jehovah's Witness with a Lutheran? You get someone who goes around the neighborhood knocking on doors, but doesn't know what to say when someone answers!

Put any notions like that about evangelism aside as you read this chapter. Robert Driver-Bishop writes, "If you were to put together a simple account of the life of Jesus, what scenes and stories would you include? What is the single theme you would use to identify Jesus? How would you organize your thoughts? Do you know someone who needs to hear the story? How would you tell it?"[2]

How would you tell it? What would you tell?

That's not legalistic; it's just being a Christian witness. Evangelism doesn't have to take the form of knocking on neighborhood doors or looking and acting like a TV evangelist. Evangelism is simply giving God glory with your life.

Faith at work

Lesley Radius is pastor of Grace Lutheran, a small mission congregation in Wildwood, Missouri. This is her first call as a Mission Developer after graduating from the Lutheran School of Theology in Chicago. Lesley has a passion for mission and evangelism.

Grace Lutheran is the result of a collaborate effort of two neighboring congregations. When Lesley was called as their pastor, she immersed herself in prayer to discover how the congregation could grow in discipleship. After much prayer, she came upon the purpose-driven model and felt that God had given her the answer.

Grace Lutheran participated in the 40 Days of Purpose campaign in September 2003. One of the main benefits of the campaign was the small group focus on the gifts people had been given by God and ways they could use those gifts to serve God and others. The congregation is well educated and financially secure with about fifty people in worship each Sunday. Lesley told me that during the 40 Days of Purpose the congregation started focusing not just on themselves, but on building their church family and on blessing the community.

Karl is a member of Grace Lutheran and experienced a real sense of calling during the 40 Days campaign. He had not been in a small group before, but he found it to be a very moving experience, and it really opened him up to a new way of following Christ. Karl said, "This experience has helped me discover a hunger for God's word to the point that in the past three years I've committed myself to three Bible studies each week." Two of those Bible studies are at work.

Karl works in information technology at a financial planning office that values community service and long-term relationships. During the 40 Days campaign at Grace Lutheran, Karl noticed a co-worker who had a copy of *The Purpose-Driven Life* on his desk. Karl struck up a conversation with him about it, and they started meeting weekly for a book study. They invited others in and then started a second weekly Bible study at the office. After they completed the book they continued to meet at the office for weekly Bible study. It was a formative part of his journey of discipleship and mission, and it opened him up to a new way of following Christ.

What vision do you believe God has for your life? What life purpose do you believe God has placed in your heart? How can you live into that purpose and then share it with others? When you spend those quiet moments on a moonlit walk with God, what does God whisper in your heart? What do you long to do, and perhaps even know that you should step out and try, but something is holding you back from following through? Maybe it's a change you need to make or maybe it's a new direction you need to go. Maybe God is calling you to reach out in faith to others, to invite or welcome them into a closer relationship with God.

Remember, you are God's workmanship, an intricate and wonderful being that God wove together in your mother's womb for a purpose. You are made in God's image as a gifted, beloved child, and there is nothing better to offer back to God than to magnify and glorify God with your entire life. You won't be saved by glorifying or magnifying God, but because you are God's child, you are called to give honor and glory to God by finishing on earth the work that God gave you to do.

Johann Sebastian Bach used to write the letters SDG at the end of his musical compositions. The letters stood for *soli deo gloria*, which means, "To God alone be the glory." Could that be the inscription at the end of your life? Could that be written on your tombstone as a summary of your life? As you look back at your life, how many of your accomplishments could be in inscribed with SDG?

Where are you focusing the energy of your life? Are you in the mode of climbing the ladder of success and accumulating titles, diplomas, and focusing your life on accumulating possessions?

There's nothing wrong with that if you see it as a growth phase. But God calls us to another level of significance that clearly has to do with a life of sacrificial giving and of sharing Christ with those who need to hear about him. Will you be a messenger of hope to help others capture a glimpse of God's vision for their lives?

You see, heaven throws a party when a new believer is welcomed into the kingdom. Read Luke 15. There's a party in heaven each time someone who is lost is found. God cares about all of us, especially sinners. Many don't realize they are lost. They don't believe they need God or the forgiveness and saving help God offers.

Will you tell them about Jesus? Don't think of it as guilt. Think of it as an opportunity to invite them to a party on their behalf.

A passionate life

Walt Kallestad and Mike Breen have written a wonderful book titled *A Passionate Life.*[3] In it they write:

> God does not expect you to be who you are not, but he does want you to be all that he has made you to be. When we know what we have been designed for and called to do, we can save ourselves a lot of striving in areas we were not built for. If we know who God has made us to be, we can stop trying to be someone we are not and let go of the stress that comes with living that kind of life. God has made you to fit in a certain place where you can serve him best, where he can shower you with grace.[4]

Fitting into a certain place where you can serve God best is fulfilling the purpose of evangelism for your life.

Breen and Kallestad write about "Presence Evangelism" and describe it in this way: "Presence Evangelism happens when you are simply present in a situation with an individual or group. Pretty obvious, really. Where you are right now is always an opportunity to model Jesus, acting as he would act, speaking as he would speak."[5]

I volunteer at my daughter's middle school every week. On Thursday mornings I spend about thirty minutes with a group of six-to-ten kids who have difficulty reading. We read through a science article, identify a who, what, where, why, when, and how, and then they summarize the article in three sentences.

After one Thursday morning with twelve sixth-graders, one of the girls talked to me as I walked them back to class. She said, "Wow, you must get paid a lot to do this." And I said, "You know, actually I volunteer to do this, so I don't get paid anything." She said, "Why would you volunteer to spend time with a bunch of middle school kids?" And I said, "I enjoy it, and besides, I think that spending time with middle school kids and teaching them is one of the purposes that God has for my life." She replied, "Wow. That's pretty cool."

The young girl may never grace the door of a Lutheran church. But it was an opportunity just to share what I believe God has called me to do. It was easy. And it may have opened a door in her life. How many people do you talk to each day who need a door opened in their life? You can do it. That's one of the purposes God has for you.

Live for the testimony

Tony Campolo tells the story of an inner-city church that had an annual high school recognition day. At one of the commencement addresses the pastor said, "Children, you're all going to die. You may not think you're going to die, but you're going to die. One of these days they're going to take you out to the cemetery, drop you into a hole, throw some dirt on your face, go back to the church and eat potato salad, and talk about you."

Then he said, "And what they say about you depends on whether you lived your life to get *titles* or *testimonies*. Will they list your degrees and awards, or will they tell about what you meant to their lives? Will they talk about all the boards you sat on and the things you owned, or will they talk about all the money you gave away that made a difference in the world? There's nothing wrong with titles. Titles are a good thing to have. But if it ever comes down to a choice between a title or a testimony, *go for the testimony."* And then he warmed up and started to preach. He said,

"Pharaoh may have had the title . . .

But Moses had the testimony!

Nebuchadnezzar may have had the title . . .

But Daniel had the testimony!

Queen Jezebel may have had the title . . .

But Elijah had the testimony!"

As he went on, getting louder and louder with each one, he finally said,

"Pilate may have had the title . . ."

And then, pausing while people knew the answer, he said,

"But my Jesus had the testimony!"

And then he asked them, "What will it be for your life?"[6]

What will it be for your life? Your personal testimony is much more effective than any sermon a pastor will ever preach. As a pastor, I'm a "paid salesman" for the Christian faith. I'm supposed to say what I say. But when we have a testimony in worship from a member of the congregation, people really listen. They listen to a sermon, they watch video clips, and they take sermon notes, but when one of them gets up to speak about the difference Christ makes in their lives, they really listen.

What is your testimony?

God has shaped you with a unique life purpose and a specific life message. Nobody but you has the gifts, abilities, passions, and desires that you have. You have a story to share, and it has a number of parts:

- First, your testimony. There's nobody anywhere that can be forced into becoming a Christian. They need to believe and accept what God wishes to give. While you can't argue someone into God's kingdom, you can tell people what happened for you and how it changed your life.
- Second, your life lessons. These are things you have learned about life simply by living closer to the way that God wants you to live. Some of these lessons may come from painful experiences you've had; in fact, some of those difficult lessons may be the best lessons you share!
- Third, things you are passionate about. What in life has affected you personally? For what need in the world does your heart beat? Consider concerns such as depression, abuse, poverty, homelessness, or any number of needs that hurt people every day. How can you make a difference?
- Fourth, the gospel. What's the good news that you can share with those around you? What part of this remarkable message can you share with someone to draw them closer to Christ?

If you were going to tell someone about the importance of your faith, where would you start? What would you want them to know about God? That's the place to start. Kelly Fryer writes:

> So you're ready to get to work doing something that really matters with your life. Or maybe you've been at it for a while but it's time for you to re-up, recommit, reenergize. And because you're so eager to get going, this may sound strange. But the place to start is *not* with you. Rather, a discussion about the meaning and purpose of our lives has to begin with *God*.[7]

If you've ever walked away from a conversation and thought to yourself, "I should have said something about my faith in God," don't miss that opportunity again. As I've said before, part of the battle starts in your mind, and requires a different perspective on life. Look for opportunities to share God's love in Christ. Make yourself available to have the Holy Spirit work in your life. And remember, "Whatever you do, in word or deed, do everything in the name of the Lord Jesus, giving thanks to God through him" (Colossians 3:17). John Wesley's rule was to do all the good you can, by all the means you can, in all the ways you can, in all the places you can, at all the times you can, to all the people you can, as long as ever you can. That's pretty good!

You can waste your life, or you can invest it. What matters is not the duration of your life, but the donation. Life is not about what you get; it's about what you give.[8] Live into the purpose for which God created you. That will truly be a life of significance, a life worth leading.

Questions for discussion

1. Jesus talked about the purpose of life five different times in five different books of the Bible. Read Matthew 28:18-20; Mark 16:15; Luke 24:47-48; John 20:21; and Acts 1:8. What are the common themes? What are the differences? Which one do you find most compelling for your life?

2. Now that we've identified the five purposes for your life in chapters 2-6, which do you experience most fully? Which one do you find most difficult?

3. If you were going to tell someone about your faith, where would you start? What would it take to do that this week? Who would you tell? Are you willing to make a commitment to doing that?

7

One More Night with the Frogs

Then Pharaoh called Moses and Aaron, and said, "Pray to the Lord to take away the frogs from me and my people, and I will let the people go to sacrifice to the Lord." Moses said to Pharaoh, "Kindly tell me when I am to pray for you and for your officials and for your people, that the frogs may be removed from you and your houses and be left only in the Nile."

And he said, "Tomorrow."

—Exodus 8:8-10

Procrastination is my sin.
It brings me naught but sorrow.
I know that I should stop it.
In fact, I will—tomorrow!

—Gloria Pitzer

Most people go to their graves with their music still inside them.

—Oliver Wendell Holmes

The Old Testament book of Exodus contains a great story that takes place during when God's chosen servant Moses sent ten plagues upon Pharaoh and the people of Egypt. There were plagues of darkness, lice, locusts, water turned into blood, and more. One of the plagues was the plague of frogs that infested the entire land. It was a huge problem for Pharaoh and the people of Egypt because there were frogs everywhere—frogs in ovens, in clothes bins, in wells. Everywhere the people turned or sat or walked, there were frogs. There were big frogs, ugly frogs, small frogs, slimy frogs, horny toad frogs, and chirping frogs everywhere. You could turn to kiss your spouse goodnight and end up kissing a frog instead!

Pharaoh called for Moses and Aaron and asked them to plead with God to take away the frog problem from the land. If they did, the Pharaoh promised to let Moses' people go. Moses said, "When do you want me to ask God to get rid of the frogs?" And Pharaoh said, "Tomorrow" (Exodus 8:10). Isn't that amazing? Pharaoh said, "Tomorrow." In essence he was saying, "Give me one more night with the frogs!"[1] Give me one more night or day with my problems. Let me deal with it tomorrow.

Even though the frogs were a huge problem, and even though they represented a curse for him and his people, Pharaoh still said, "Tomorrow. Give me one more night with the frogs." Why not get rid of the frogs right now? Why not deal with your problems and issues today, instead of tomorrow?

Why? Because it's human nature. Why deal today with something you can deal with tomorrow? Why deal with some of your problems, your regrets, your insecurities, or your issues today when you can do it tomorrow? Has it ever happened to you that you could deal with some of the challenges in your life today, but instead, you say, "Tomorrow? Give me one more night with my frogs, my struggles, my challenges, and my problems?"

I'll start reading my Bible more. And I'll start tomorrow for sure. I'm really going to start loving my spouse more. Tomorrow seems to be a good day to do it. I'll get involved in ministry more frequently at church. But not until next week.

At www.despair.com there's a link that's devoted to the fine art of procrastination. The site calls them "de-motivators," and they provide little cards, notes, and posters that you can put up in your office to de-motivate you. One of them reads, "Procrastinate: Hard work pays off over time, but laziness pays off immediately."

We Christians are no different. When tomorrow comes, we may say the same thing all over again, and make the same tomorrow commitments. Sometimes we get mad at God and say, "God, why are there all these frogs in my life? Why do I have these struggles? And why don't you do something about them?"

The story of Pharaoh's tomorrow teaches us that procrastination precedes tribulation and trials. When you keep putting things off you're setting yourself up for trouble. God doesn't want you to delay, but wants you to do what you already know you should do.

Pharaoh finally lost everything before he finally said YES to what God (through Moses) wanted him to do. He endured all kinds of pain and plagues, including the death of his own son. His kingdom was devastated. He finally obeyed when the tribulation was allowed to go full force.

How long are you going to wait? What is it going to take? Pharaoh was waiting to see if he could do it on his own without God. He was buying time to see if his magicians could cause the frogs to die under their spells. He wanted to do it without God. But you need God. You can't do it on your own. You cannot achieve or attain significance without God. You were not meant to do things without God. Don't wait until your life falls apart, your family is destroyed, your sanity is stretched to the brink, and your health is ruined before you start responding to God's call on your life.

Being a Christian means that those who believe in Jesus must get fed up with the frogs in their lives. There must come a day when you have absolutely no tolerance for the curse of sin, death, guilt, and shame in your life. As a new creation in Christ the power of life has more power over you than the power of sin and death. It means that you need to change your perspective on life to see God present and active in leading your life.

An A-B-C process

How can you make that change? At the risk of being too simplistic, let me describe an A-B-C process that is very straightforward. It is better known in more evangelical circles than in most traditional Lutheran circles.

First, *accept.* Accept God's love for you. Remember that the Bible promises that there is nothing in all of creation that is able to separate you from the love of God in Jesus Christ, our Lord. There is nothing that can separate you—no frogs, no problems, no struggles. Nothing in your past can separate you from God's love. Simply accept that God loves you.

Second, *believe.* Believe that Jesus lived his life *for you* and died on the cross *for you* and came back to life *for you.* Believe that when the pastor says, "This is Christ's body and blood, given and shed *for you,* that it really is *for you.* Believe that Jesus extends his arms to embrace you because he loves you and gave his life *for you.*

Third, *commit.* Commit to making the love of God and the sacrifice of Jesus more real in your life. Commit to reading the Bible more often, to coming to church more regularly, to discovering more about prayer, and to living your life more closely aligned with what God wants you to be doing.

Quitters, campers, and climbers

Paul Stoltz has a book titled *The Adversity Quotient: Turning Obstacles into Opportunities.*[2] He suggests that an important ability in life is to be able to bounce back from obstacles and move forward. What is most important is a person's perception and their response to obstacles and adversities, rather than the obstacle or adversity itself. He says that challenges can be like climbing a mountain and suggests three responses that people have when they are faced with an obstacle that seems insurmountable.

First, some people become quitters. They just quit and go back home. When faced with the odds against them, some people just shut down and quit. Instead of climbing the mountain, or facing the challenge of frogs in their lives, some people just deal with it by quitting.

Second, some people become campers. When faced with adversity, some people decide to become campers. The put up their tents and stay where they are, rather than quit or move ahead. So they stay there in limbo, not facing the challenge, deciding not to deal with it.

Pharaoh was a camper. Take the frogs out of my life tomorrow.

Third, some people become climbers. Stoltz says that climbers see adversity or frogs in their lives as limited, as external, and as something that can be conquered. Climbers do not let adversity set up a base camp in their lives. Instead, they move forward with no patience for the frogs.

Take a moment and read through John 20:1-18. You'll see these three kinds of people. The disciples ran to the empty tomb when Mary told them about it. They looked in and saw the empty grave clothes, they believed, and then we read these words: "Then they returned to their homes" (John 20:10). They had just seen Jesus overcome the greatest obstacle of all time, and yet they returned to their homes! They quit. In fact, they were still in their homes a week later with the door shut in fear. They simply gave up and quit.

Mary, however, didn't just quit and go home. Instead, she became a camper. She stayed at the door of the tomb and saw the angels there. She didn't understand what was really happening, but she stayed where she was and camped at the door of the tomb.

She camped there until she met the risen Jesus. She saw him at the tomb but didn't recognize him. In fact, she thought he was the gardener. But then something important happened.

Jesus spoke her name.

All of a sudden, when she heard her name from Jesus' lips, her world changed. She climbed out of the depths of despair. She climbed into the new life that Jesus had promised her, and she ran and told the disciples that she had seen the Lord. She wasn't a quitter. She was a temporary camper. But she climbed past the obstacles that lay in front of her and into the new life that Jesus had in store for her.

Through the prophet Isaiah, God said to the people of Israel: "I have called you by name, you are mine" (Isaiah 43:1). Christians who know Jesus should have no room for frogs in their lives. A life worth leading is one where we live with purpose and passion for what God wants to do in and through us. Passionate Christians would rather fail at something they love than have some success at something for which they have no passion.

God meant *this* February

During Lent of 2003 we did the 40 Days of Purpose campaign at St. Matthew. We did it almost half-heartedly and didn't do all the bells and whistles that the campaign calls for (we should have done them). The following summer we did a sermon series called "Dare to Dream" focusing on the dreams and passions that God puts in our hearts, and the importance of responding to those dreams.[3]

At the beginning of November of that year a wonderful, passionate retired missionary in our congregation who spent more than thirty years in Africa came to me and said, "Pastor Eric, God has laid on my heart to gather a group of ten people from St. Matthew and take them to Tanzania for a month's mission work, and we'd like to do that in February." I said, "Well, Bob, that's a pretty big undertaking, but I think you could probably pull it off in fifteen months." But Bob said, "No, I mean we'd leave in three months. *This* February."

Now, I know that we'd been preaching about discovering your life's purpose, drawing closer to God's heart, and daring to dream. I know that I had been preaching that it's better to fail at something than to not even try. But I was also just about 99.9 percent convinced that God needed more than three months to pull off a month-long mission trip to Africa. I wondered whether Bob was just suffering from indigestion from too many fish tacos the night before. But Bob was pretty insistent that this was a calling from God, and he just needed my affirmation to go ahead and start to recruit.

Well, it was amazing, or should I say that God was amazing. Within a month Bob had his entire team assembled. Within six weeks he had the funding for the trip, including an incredible deal on plane tickets and some generous funding from our congregation's recent capital campaign that we had designated for benevolence like this. The group left for Tanzania three months after our conversation. Since this first trip, Bob has organized two more month-long trips, several others have gone on their own, we provided monies to fund three college students on their own mission trips to faraway places, I have been to Tanzania on a World Vision trip, and my associate, Jim Doherty, has also been to Tanzania. We've started to make some important connections between St. Matthew and Tanzania.

It was my mistake. God meant *this* February.

But it isn't all about our own passion. It's tied in to Jesus' passion. Remember, it's not about you, it's about God. Erwin McManus writes:

> While a common definition of passion is "a compelling emotion or desire," the most unusual definition of passion is the suffering of Christ on the cross. . . . It is not incidental that the death of Jesus has come to be known as the Passion. The cross of Jesus Christ points to everything that God is passionate about. God the Son so passionately loves humanity that he was willing to give his own life in our behalf. You know what you are really passionate about when you are willing to lay your life down for it.[4]

What are you willing to lay your life down for? What idea or concept are you willing to give your life for? You have music in your heart: Is it still strong and playing, or did it die long ago? What can you do to rediscover it and play it at full volume in your life?

What holds you back? Do you have frogs in your life? Frogs of resentment about something your spouse didn't do or about a friend who hasn't called? Frogs of fear that strike terror into your heart? Frogs of guilt and shame that keep sadness in your soul? Far too often we just live with those things and put up with them day after day without calling on God to banish them forever. We live one more night with the frogs.

Give up the cheese and crackers

Think of it this way. There was a very poor man years ago who wanted to travel to the United States from Europe on a cruise ship. He worked hard, saved every penny he could, and finally he had enough money to buy a ticket to board the ship. It was about a two-week trip, so before he left he went out and bought a suitcase and filled it with cheese and crackers. That's all he could afford. Once on board, all the other passengers went to the large, ornate dining room to eat their gourmet meals. Meanwhile the poor man would go over in the corner and eat his cheese and crackers. This went on day after day. He could smell the delicious food being served in the dining room. He heard the other passengers speak of it in glowing terms as they rubbed their bellies and complained about how full they were and how they would have to go one a diet after the trip. The poor traveler wanted to join the other guests and the dining room, but he had no extra money. Sometimes he would lie awake at night, dreaming of the sumptuous meals the other guests described.

Toward the end of the trip, another man came up to him and said "Sir, I can't help but notice that you were always over there eating those cheese and crackers at mealtime. Why don't you come to the banquet hall with us?"

The traveler's face flushed with embarrassment, and he said, "Well, to tell you the truth, I only had enough money to buy the ticket. I didn't have any extra money to purchase fancy meals." The other passenger raised his eyebrows in surprise. He shook his head and said, "Sir, didn't you realize the meals were included in the price of the ticket? Your meals have already been paid for."[5]

Think of that in terms of our faith. God has all ready given us incredible gifts and blessed us with spiritual blessings. Jesus gave you the greatest gift of all, the gift of forgiveness and new life. It's incredible. But instead of receiving it with joy, far too many of us sit alone in the corner, away from the banquet of blessings, eating our cheese and crackers.

Isn't it time for no more cheese and crackers? Shouldn't this be your last night with the frogs? Receive the gifts of love, grace, and encouragement that God wishes to give you. Live into the purpose God has for your life. It's time.

Questions for discussion

1. What are some of the things that you put off until tomorrow that you know you should do today? What is keeping you from doing them?

2. What has procrastination meant in your life? Have you missed any opportunities because of it? What can you do to make sure you capture the opportunities God places in front of you?

3. What frogs do you have in your life? What are you going to do about them?

4. Think about the A-B-C process. Write down what you accept, what you believe, and what you commit to do. How might doing this change your life?

8

A Life Worth Leading

Be careful then how you live, not as unwise people but as wise, making the most of the time, because the days are evil.
So do not be foolish, but understand what the will of the Lord is.
—Ephesians 5:15-16

Deep in the heart of love, there beats an "ought."
—Gerhard Frost

I therefore, the prisoner in the Lord, beg you to lead a life worthy of the calling to which you have been called.
—Ephesians 4:1

When I was in grade school, I absolutely loved it when my mom would bake chocolate chip cookies from scratch. There was nothing better than sneaking into the kitchen and taking a warm, gooey cookie off the rack and eating it with a glass of cold milk. Sometimes when I would come home from school she would be right in the middle of baking those cookies. When the windows to the house were open, the incredible smell of baking cookies drifted outside, and I knew even before I opened the door that the cookies were being baked.

I loved the warm cookies, but I loved the brown sugar dough with hidden chocolate chips even more. To me, the cookies tasted the worst when the cookies were taken out of the oven too soon and they were in that transition stage between being dough and cookie. In my opinion, half-baked chocolate chip cookies aren't worth much.

It is that same way with most things that begin with the word *half*. Almost always something that is "half" describes something that is incomplete. Half-baked is neither good for chocolate chip cookies, nor for an idea or concept. Half-done refers to having as much to do in the future as you've already completed. Half-dead is never the look you want to have when you go off to start the day. Half-alive makes you wonder which half. Half-price makes you wonder what's wrong with it. Half-crazy means that you're just sane enough to be out on the streets, but not much more.

I sometimes wonder how many Christians live with a half-hearted faith that results in a half-hearted life. We probably don't know each other, but you bought this book for a reason. I call it a purpose. If you're wondering about living a life worth leading, then we share a common vision about life. I care about you and want this book to be a blessing for your life.

I mentioned in the introduction there are several ways to use this book. You may have read this book just for your own purpose, and now you may be considering reading it with a small group at church or work. If you're a pastor you may consider using this book as a sermon series with small group discussions. Look at the worship resources at www.alifeworthleading.org to see how other churches have used the book this way. There are also some very valuable resources that complement the direction of this book that are available at that site.

A whisper from God

In reading this book you probably have picked up on the kinds of books I like to read. One of the books I skimmed through was a bestseller by Po Bronson titled *What Should I Do With My Life? The True Story of People Who Answered the Ultimate Question*.[1] He traveled around the country interviewing individuals ". . . who have struggled to find their calling, their true nature—people who made mistakes before getting it right." [2] He writes, "We all have passions if we choose to see them. Most of us don't get epiphanies. We don't get clarity. Our purpose doesn't arrive neatly packaged as destiny. We only get a whisper. A blank, nonspecific urge. That's how it starts."[3]

I like what he says, or at least I thought I did. But as I skimmed through the book I noticed virtually no reference to God, Jesus, or the Holy Spirit. There's no mention of the Great Commandment or the Great Commission. What good is the purpose of your life if it's whispered from your rebellious sinful nature? What good is the purpose if it's from indigestion or from a self-serving goal? What good is it if it's about us and not God? Without God the purpose for your life is like being out in the ocean, not seeing the shore, and starting to swim anyway. If you don't know where you're ultimately going, any path you take will get you there.

Knowing God makes all the difference in the world. It means that you may be in the ocean, but you can see the shore, and you know that God can help you get there. It's realizing that the purpose of your life is to love God and love others.

A whisper from God can start you on your path toward purpose.

A life worth leading

Ephesians 4 begins with these words: "I therefore, the prisoner in the Lord, beg you to lead a life worthy of the calling to which you have been called, with all humility and gentleness, with patience, bearing with one another in love, making every effort to maintain the unity of the Spirit in the bond of peace" (Ephesians 4:1-3).

Notice the *therefore*. The writer encourages the Ephesians to lead a life worthy of the calling to which they had been called based on what the author had said previously in the first three chapters.

In *Consequences: Morality, Ethics, and the Future,* James Burtness writes:

The first three chapters of Ephesians are verbal symphony of praise to the cosmic drama of the God of creation and redemption working through Jesus the crucified and risen Lord to accomplish God's purpose for all things and all peoples. There follows a distinct pause, after which the reader can almost hear the wild applause. Then comes the unmistakable "therefore." Since this is what God has done and is doing and will do, and since God has called you into the fellowship of believers, it follows that you should "lead a life worthy of the calling to which you have been called" (Ephesians 4:1). The connection drawn between believing and behaving is decisive and dramatic.[4]

That pattern is repeated in other places in the Bible. Paul presents the Christian faith with articulate clarity in the first eleven chapters of Romans. He builds an airtight case for the lostness of humanity and the necessity for God to intervene for our salvation. He proclaims God's endless love and the freedom from law and sin that characterizes the Christian life. He clearly says that our works will do nothing to gain favor with God. It's all about God.

The "therefore" comes in chapter 12, after proclaiming the work of Christ for eleven chapters. "I appeal to you *therefore,* brothers and sisters, by the mercies of God, to present your bodies as a living sacrifice, holy and acceptable to God, which is your spiritual worship" (Romans 12:1-2).

The pattern is repeated in the first several chapters of Colossians, which tell of a Cosmic Christ as the image of the invisible God. "For in him all the fullness of God was pleased to dwell, and through him God was pleased to reconcile to himself all things, whether on earth or in heaven, by making peace through the blood of the cross" (Colossians 1:20). Then comes the *therefore* about how we should live our lives: "As you therefore have received Christ Jesus the Lord, continue to live your lives in him. . . . And whatever you do, in word or deed, do everything in the name of the Lord

Jesus, giving thanks to God the Father through him" (Colossians 2:6, 3:17).

The pattern is even more tightly connected in other verses. "In this is love, not that we loved God but that he loved us and sent his Son to be the atoning sacrifice for our sins. Beloved, since God loves us so much, we also ought to love one another" (1 John 4:10-11). God takes the initiative and we are asked to respond. The pattern is important, as it is God's action. We receive the gifts that God so graciously wishes to give. And we respond with lives of faith and love.

The Sermon on the Mount begins with a magnificent description of the blessed life. "Blessed are the poor in spirit, for theirs is the kingdom of heaven. Blessed are those who mourn, for they will be comforted" (Matthew 5:3-4). The Beatitudes describe the life that God so graciously gives us. Following the Beatitudes Jesus calls us to give glory to God by the way we live: "You are the light of the world. A city built on a hill cannot be hid. No one after lighting a lamp puts it under the bushel basket, but on the lamp stand, and it gives light to all in the house. In the same way, let your light shine before others, so that they may see your good works and give glory to your Father in heaven" (Matthew 5:14-16).

God wants your whole life, not just an hour on Sunday morning. God wants to walk with you in everything you say and do. We often manage our time by segmenting the hours of the day and dividing our time between work, sleep, recreation, family, shopping, cleaning, and the multitude of other activities that fill our day. Church, prayer, and devotions often fill a minor percent of those segments.

A life worth leading is one that finds room for those things that strengthen faith and encourage faithful living. Like a shower of grace, a life worth leading lavishly splashes the name Jesus over each part of life. A life worth leading recognizes the unique purpose to which God calls you. A life worth leading is one that embraces that purpose in everything you do. God wants your whole life, not just certain portions of it.

C. S. Lewis said the only thing that Christianity can't be is moderately important. It must invade everything in your life. That means being open to change and renewal; it means living with a sense of expectation. With all the things that compete for our time and energy, leading a life focused on God's purpose can be a monumental task that takes will and commitment. Living with passion and purpose is not for the faint of heart, but it is a deeply significant way to follow Jesus in word and deed.

Give me the mountain

Remember the story of Caleb from chapter 1? Once again, I ask you to think about where you are. Are you in captivity, wandering in the wilderness, or on your way to the Promised Land? Let's pick up the second part of the story of Caleb, which continues in Joshua 14:6.

The people of Israel had been wandering in the wilderness for forty years. All of the older generations had died except for Joshua and Caleb. In Joshua 14:6-12, they are splitting up the territory of the Promised Land. Caleb makes his plea for the portion of the Promised Land that he and his descendents would inherit. Caleb recalls forty years ago how he brought back an honest report to Moses, and God promised that he would be the only one to inherit the land because he followed the Lord wholeheartedly. Caleb, now eighty-five years old, says, "I am still as strong today as I was on the day that Moses sent me; my strength now is as my strength was then, for war, and for going and coming. So now give me this hill country of which the LORD spoke on that day; for you heard on that day how the Anakim were there, with great fortified cities; it may be that the Lord will be with me, and I shall drive them out, as the LORD said" (Joshua 14:11-12).

Like the famous line from the movie *Jerry McGuire,* "Show me the money!" Caleb says, "Give me the mountain!"

The Anakim, the huge giants that caused the ten spies to give a negative report forty years before, lived in those mountains. When the ten spies saw the Anakim, they felt that they were themselves as insignificant as grasshoppers. But Caleb, now age eighty-five and claiming the strength of the Lord, wants the mountain. No grasshopper complex for Caleb; he has a different spirit because he followed God wholeheartedly.

Give me the mountain. That's where the biggest challenges and struggles (and rewards) are. That's what caused the others to fail and retreat in fear, but not Caleb. He moved forward in faith. Caleb's life and faith teach us that, when we compare ourselves to the mountain-ous tasks that lie in front of us, we will always fall short because we will only be relying on ourselves. The question is this: "Am I willing invite God to go with me, work through me, and conquer whatever moun-tain lies ahead?" Caleb wholeheartedly followed God's purpose for his life. He could have been discouraged because of his age, but he had a heart for God. He knew that he was able to accomplish all things only through God who strengthened him. He knew his purpose in life.

Will you focus on your grasshopper abilities or will you focus on the promise and the purpose that God has for you? Will you ask for the mountain in your life or will you settle for a "just good enough" life? Will you face the challenges of living as a grasshopper? Or, like Caleb, will you embrace God's purpose for your life? The choice, by God's grace, is yours.

Let me close with a prayer, attributed to St. Patrick:

The Rising
Let us go forth,
In the goodness of our merciful Father,
In the gentleness of our Brother Jesus,
In the radiance of his Holy Spirit,
In the faith of the apostles,
In the joyful praise of the angels,

In the holiness of the saints,
In the courage of the martyrs.

Let us go forth
In the wisdom of our all-seeing Father,
In the patience of our all-loving Brother,
In the truth of the all-knowing Spirit,
In the learning of the apostles,
In the gracious guidance of the angels,
In the patience of the saints,
In the self control of the martyrs.

Such is the path for all servants of Christ,
The path from death to eternal life.[5]

Choose the path of a life worth leading. May God bless your journey.

Questions for discussion

1. How do you take time to hear what God is "whispering to you"? What is God whispering in your ear recently?

2. How would you relate to Jesus' words, "you are the light of the world," to living a life worth leading?

3. Are you ready to say, "Give me the mountain"? If yes, why now? If no, what holds you back?

Dedication

This book is dedicated to my older brother, Steve, who died an untimely death in February 2005. Steve was a wonderful brother to my sister, brother, and me. He was a great son to my parents. Being manic depressive brought him many challenges. But he had a wonderful spirit, an awesome memory, and a great sense of humor. St. Anthony Park Lutheran was full to the brim as we commended him to Almighty God who claimed him at the time of his baptism and who guided him each day of his life. The community, Gingko's, Speedy Market, the seminary faculty, and family and friends gathered to wish this precious soul Godspeed on his way to eternal life.

Steve was one of the reasons I entered seminary. I felt called to influence people's lives in a way that brought them closer to the reason and purpose for which God had created them. In the end, Steve taught those who knew and loved him that the primary purpose for us being here is to love God and love others with every fiber of our being. Steve did both of those exceptionally well.

Endnotes

Introduction

1. Harold Kushner, *When All You've Ever Wanted Isn't Enough* (New York: Summit Books, 1986), 8.

2. Katie Brazelton, *Pathway to Purpose for Women* (Grand Rapids, Mich.: Zondervan, 2005), 19.

3. James Emery White, *You Can Experience a Purposeful Life* (Nashville: Word Publishing, 2000), 2.

4. Kelly Fryer, *No Experience Necessary* (Minneapolis: Augsburg Fortress, 2005).

5. Eric Burtness, *Leading on Purpose: Intentionality and Teaming in Congregational Life* (Minneapolis: Augsburg Fortress, 2004).

Chapter 1: The Power of Purpose

1. Rick Warren, *The Purpose-Driven Life: What On Earth Am I Here For?* (Grand Rapids, Mich.: Zondervan, 2002).

2. Ibid., 103-109.

3. Ibid., jacket cover.

4. Ibid., 17.

5. Kelly Fryer, *No Experience Necessary: Unit 2: You're Hired* (Minneapolis: Augsburg Fortress, 2005), 103

6. Ibid., 103-104. Article 6 of the Augsburg Confession is "Concerning the New Obedience" which says that "such a faith should yield good fruit and good works and that a person must do such good works as God has commanded for God's sake but not place trust in them as thereby to earn grace from God."

7. Michael W. Foss, *Real Faith for Real Life: Living the Six Marks of Discipleship* (Minneapolis: Augsburg Fortress, 2004).

Chapter 2: Worship

1. Fryer, *You're Hired*, 85.

2. Foss, 39.

3. Warren, 65.

4. Ibid., 66.

5. Ibid., 77.

6. Adapted from "On Courage" in Chicken Soup for the Soul, written and compiled by Jack Canfield and Mark Victor Hansen, (Deerfield Beach, Fla.: Health Communications, Inc., 1993), 27-28.

7. Robert Driver-Bishop, *People of Purpose: 40 Life Lessons from the New Testament* (Minneapolis: Augsburg Fortress, 2005), 25.

8. From Rick Warren's Sermon, Week 2 of the 40 Days of Purpose Campaign.

Chapter 3: Fellowship

1. Christine and Tom Sine, *Living on Purpose: Finding God's Best for your Life* (Grand Rapids, Mich.: Baker Books, 2002), 142.

2. Jeffrey Paul Whillock, *Grow Groups: Nurturing Discipleship through Short-Term Small Groups Centered on the Sunday Scripture and Sermon* (A thesis submitted to the faculty of Luther Theological Seminary in partial fulfillment of the requirements for the Degree of Doctor of Ministry, Mary E. Hess, Thesis Advisor, St. Paul, Minn., 2003), 1.

3. Ibid., 23.

4. *The Small Catechism by Martin Luther in Contemporary English* (Minneapolis: Augsburg Publishing House, 1960, 1968).

Chapter 4: Discipleship

1. *Lutheran Book of Worship* (Minneapolis: Augsburg; Philadelphia: Board of Publication, Lutheran Church in America, 1978), 74, 94, 117 (author's emphasis).

2. From *Renewing Worship 6: Holy Communion and Related Rites* (Evangelical Lutheran Church in America, 2004), 6.

3. Summarized from Rick Warren's preaching workshop material.

4. David W. Anderson and Paul Hill, *Frogs Without Legs Can't Hear: Nurturing Disciples in Home and Congregation* (Minneapolis: Augsburg Fortress, 2003).

5. Ibid., 11.

Chapter 5: Ministry
1. Thomas O. Chisholm, b. 1866, C. Harold Lowden, *Living for Jesus*, 19th cent.
2. Robert Driver-Bishop, *People of Purpose: 40 Life Lessons from the New Testament* (Minneapolis: Augsburg Fortress, 2005), 101.
3. John Ortberg, *If You Want to Walk on Water, You've Got to Get out of the Boat* (Grand Rapids, Mich.: Zondervan, 2001)

Chapter 6: Evangelism
1. Rick Warren, *The Purpose-Driven Life: What On Earth Am I Here For?* (Grand Rapids, Mich.: Zondervan, 2002).
2. Driver-Bishop, 116.
3. Mike Breen and Walt Kallestad, *A Passionate Life* (Colorado Springs: Cook Communication Ministries, 2005).
4. Ibid., 135.
5. Ibid., 219.
6. Adapted from Tony Campolo, *Who Switched the Price Tags? A Search for Values in a Mixed-up World* (Waco, Tex.: Word, 1986), 29.
7. Kelly Fryer, *No Experience Necessary: Unit One: Help Wanted* (Minneapolis: Augsburg Fortress, 2005), 21.
8. These three statements are used in multiple places in Purpose Driven material.

Chapter 7: One More Night with the Frogs
1. There are several sermons available online with this title.
2. Paul Stoltz, *The Adversity Quotient: Turning Obstacles into Opportunities* (New York: John Wiley & Sons, Inc, 1997), 14-15.
3. You can read more about these in my book *Leading on Purpose: Intentionality and Teaming in Congregational Life* (Minneapolis: Augsburg Fortress, 2004) in the Lutheran Voices Series. You can also see more at www.leadingonpurpose.org and at www.alifeworthleading.org.
4. Erwin Raphael McManus, *Uprising—A Revolution of the Soul* (Nashville: Thomas Nelson, 2003), 24.
5. Paraphrased from Joel Osteen, *Your Best Life Now* (New York: Time Warner Faith, 2004), 83-86.

Chapter 8: A Life Worth Leading

1. Po Bronson, *What Should I Do with My Life? The True Story of People Who Answered the Ultimate Question* (Random House: New York, 2002).

2. Ibid., inside front book cover.

3. Ibid.

4. James H. Burtness, *Consequences: Morality, Ethics, and the Future* (Fortress Press: Minneapolis, 1999), 143.

5. As found in *Celtic Fire* (New York: Doubleday, 1991), 143, a Celtic evening hymn traditionally attributed to Patrick.

Other Resources from Augsburg

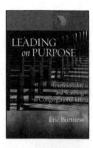

Leading on Purpose by Eric Burtness
96 pages, 0-8066-5174-1

Exploring the Purpose-Driven Church phenomenon,
Eric Burtness provides pastors and church leaders with a
Lutheran view of what it means to lead on purpose and
integrates the Purpose-Driven philosophy into the context
of Lutheran congregational life.

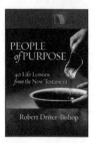

People of Purpose by Robert Driver-Bishop
128 pages, 0-8066-4936-4

This book explores forty New Testament people and the themes
that emerge from their stories. It helps readers to grow and
mature in the faith by engaging in these themes from a "purpose" perspective.

Reclaiming the "L" Word by Kelly Fryer
96 pages, 0-8066-4596-2

Reclaiming the "L" Word is a book about renewing congregations
by recognizing and living out the core teachings of the Lutheran
faith. Inspirational, engaging, and challenging, this book is a
must-read for pastors and congregational leaders!

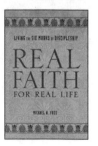

Real Faith for Real Life by Michael W. Foss
136 pages, 0-8066-4801-5

For Christians seeking to apply their faith to everyday life, *Real
Faith for Real Life* invites readers to answer the call of discipleship
and provides guidance and examples of how to do so successfully.

Available wherever books are sold.